DEMOCRACY
AFTER **LIBERALISM**

DEMOCRACY
AFTER LIBERALISM

pragmatism and deliberative politics

ROBERT B. TALISSE

Routledge
New York • London

Published in 2005 by
Routledge
270 Madison Avenue
New York, NY 10016
www.routledge-ny.com

Published in Great Britain by
Routledge
2 Park Square
Milton Park, Abington
Oxon OX14 4RN
www.routledge.co.uk

Copyright © 2005 by Taylor & Francis Group, a Division of T&F Informa.
Routledge is an imprint of the Taylor & Francis Group.

Printed in the United States of America on acid-free paper.

10 9 8 7 6 5 4 3 2 1

Library of Congress Cataloging-in-Publication Data
    Talisse, Robert B.
      Democracy after liberalism : pragmatism and deliberative politics /
    Robert B. Talisse.
        p. cm.
      Includes bibliographical references and index.
      ISBN 0-415-95018-X (hb : alk. paper) — ISBN 0-415-95019-8 (pb : alk.
    paper)
        1. Liberalism. 2. Democracy. I. Title.

      JC574.T35 2004
      321.8--dc22   2004008431

For Joanne, Again

Table of Contents

Acknowledgments

First things first. I began thinking seriously about democracy and liberalism while completing my graduate work in philosophy at the City University of New York. My efforts then were especially influenced by my teachers, Steven Cahn, Virginia Held, and Peter Simpson. I thank each of them for their encouragement and continuing guidance.

The bulk of the manuscript was written during my first two summers at Vanderbilt University. I extend my deep gratitude to Brooke Ackerly, William James Booth, Mark Brandon, Bob Ehman, John Goldberg, Lenn Goodman, Steve Hetcher, John Lachs, John Post, Henry Teloh, Jeffrey Tlumak, and John Weymark, all of whom either commented on parts of the manuscript or were generous enough to engage in extended conversation about the issues dealt with herein.

Many other colleagues, students, and friends were kind enough to critically comment on parts of the manuscript, and for this, I am in their debt: Scott Aikin, Stefan Baumrin, Allen Coates, Michael Eldridge, William Galston, Dwight Goodyear, D. Micah Hester, Angelo Juffras, Chris King, Cheryl Misak, John O'Connor, Gregory Pappas, John Peterman, and Steve Ross. Thanks are due also to Bruce Ackerman, James Fishkin, Jeffrey Friedman, and Illya Somin who provided crucial support and sound advice in the final stages of preparation of the manuscript. I am especially grateful for the assistance provided by Caleb Clanton, who helped me prepare the manuscript and raised some important critical considerations just as the final version was being completed. Finally, I thank Robert Tempio, my editor at Routledge, who did a splendid job in bringing this book to completion.

I dedicate this book to my wife, Joanne Billett, to whom I owe more than I can express.

CHAPTER 1
Introduction

Democracy at the Turn of the Century

"The day of the dictator is over." So claimed President George Bush in a 1990 address in Argentina.[1] In his optimism, Bush echoed Francis Fukuyama, who had written months earlier that with the collapse of the Berlin Wall, the world had finally reached "the end point of mankind's ideological evolution" (1989, 4). More recently, political scientist Robert Dahl has expressed a similar sentiment. According to Dahl, "the main antidemocratic regimes of the twentieth century"—he refers to Communism, Fascism, and Nazism— have either "disappeared in the ruins of calamitous war" or else "collapsed from within" (1998, 1). In a less rhetorical, but no less prophetic mode than Bush and Fukuyama, Dahl explains:

> Before it ended, the twentieth century had turned into an age of democratic triumph. The global range and influence of democratic ideas, institutions, and practices had made that century far and away the most flourishing period for democracy in human history. (1998, 145)

Throughout the United States and Western Europe, the collapse of nondemocratic states and the trend toward the "universalization of Western liberal democracy as the final form of human government" (Fukuyama 1989, 4) was duly celebrated. By the final decade of the twentieth century, it seemed that Woodrow Wilson's image of a world "safe for democracy" had been realized.[2]

The optimism and mood of self-congratulation that emerged out of the close of the Cold War has lapsed in the intervening years. Despite the undeniable global ascendancy of the language of democracy, recent events suggest that we now face an international scene in which antidemocratic forces such as nationalism, tribalism, and fanaticism are rising, once again, to dangerous levels.[3] Dahl acknowledges that "even dictators appear to believe that an indispensable ingredient for their legitimacy is a dash or two of the language of democracy" (1989, 2). Picking up on this theme, Ian Shapiro observes that today "the democratic idea is close to nonnegotiable" (2003, 1). Agreeing with Shapiro, Jeffrey Stout notes that "nearly every nation makes grand democratic pronouncements nowadays" (2004, 4). Henry Richardson adds, "In all parts of the world, the trappings of democracy abound, yet nowhere is it credible to believe that the people rule" (2002, 3). We live in an age of increasing democratization (Zakaria 2003), but could it be that the global triumph of democracy is merely a triumph of democratic rhetoric?

The status of democracy at home is also uncertain. We are currently experiencing an undeniable rash of "civic privatism" (Ackerman and Fishkin 2003, 8). Robert Bellah laments, "Since the end of the Cold War, what little seemed to be holding us together is coming apart at the seams" (1999, 13). The research of sociologists and political scientists confirms Walter Lippmann's image of a bewildered, disconnected, uninformed, and apathetic public (Weinshall 2003). For example, barely half of the eligible voters cast a ballot in the 1996 presidential election (Anderson 1998, 486) and merely 51 percent voted in the 2000 (Patterson 2002, 4). Well-known studies by Robert Putman (1995; 2000) reveal a sharp pattern of decline in public participation of all varieties: voting, membership in political parties, labor unions, and school-based organizations; even newspaper reading is waning. "America is becoming a nation of emphatically private citizens—customers and clients who find it difficult to express coherent, common interests through collective political action" (Crenson and Ginsberg 2002, 234).

As one might expect, this decline in participation in political activities is accompanied by an increase of ignorance with regard to the most fundamental aspects of the workings of American government. As one researcher has put it, "Nothing strikes the student of public opinion and democracy more forcefully than the paucity of information most people possess about politics" (Ferejohn 1990, 3). In a recent article, Illya Somin provides a lucid survey of recent findings which demonstrate that ignorance is so widespread among the American public that voters "not only cannot choose between specific competing policy programs, but also cannot accurately assign credit and blame for highly visible policy outcomes to the right office-holders" (1998, 417). Bruce Ackerman and James Fishkin summarize these points nicely, "If six decades of modern public opinion research established anything, it is that the public's most basic political knowledge is appalling by any normative standard" (2003, 11). We hence confront what Anthony Giddens calls the "paradox of democracy":

> Democracy is spreading around the world . . . yet in the mature democracies, which the rest of the word is supposed to be copying, there is widespread disillusionment with democratic processes. In most Western countries, levels of trust in politicians have dropped over the past years. Fewer people turn out to vote than used to, particularly in the U.S. More and more people say that are uninterested in parliamentary politics, especially among the younger generation. Why are citizens in democratic countries apparently becoming disillusioned with democratic government, at the same time as it is spreading round the rest of the world? (2000, 90)

It seems ironic that these conditions should prevail at a time when the country has witnessed an explosion of information and communicative technologies. We arguably are living under technological conditions that are ideal for democracy. To cite a most obvious example, the Internet has vastly expanded our democratic potential. Citizens enjoy access to information and news, opportunity for the exchange of ideas and the expression of opinion, and occasion for participation in public discussion and deliberation on an unprecedented scale. Indeed, Robert Paul Wolff's once fanciful and utopian proposal for instant direct democracy via electronic voting (1970, 34–37) is now at least a technological possibility. Hence the burgeoning literature on "tele" and "cyber" democracy (Morris 2000; Wilhelm 2000; Tsagarousianou, ed. 1998).

Yet our technological facility is not often put in the service of democracy. Today, the citizen regularly confronts opinion polling, which arguably does as much to generate public opinion as to register it (Chomsky 1997, 17–29; Chomsky 1989, 45f.; Page 1996; Iyengar 2000), knee-jerk "sound off" platforms and television confessionals, which discourage rather than foster reasoned discourse, and a complex of mass media whose power to direct and divert public attention steadily increases (Anderson 1998; Kellner 1990; Iyengar 1991; Norris 2000). We face a "democracy of sound bites" (Goodin 2003, 177). According to Ackerman and Fishkin,

> We have a public dialogue that is ever more efficiently segmented in its audiences and moralized in its sound bites. We have an ever more tabloid news agenda dulling the sensitivities of an increasingly inattentive citizenry. And we have mechanisms of feedback from the public, from view call-ins to self-selected Internet polls that emphasize intense constituencies, unrepresentative of the public at large. (2003, 8)

Even the Internet, which seems to offer the promise of the unmediated communication of information and ideas, has yet to realize its democratic potentialities. In an important recent study of the political dimension of the Internet, Cass Sunstein warns that the new technology is most often used as a filtering device; the Web allows citizens to select in advance what they see and hear, thereby narrowing their perceptions of the spectrum of reasonable political debate and drastically reducing the frequency with which citizens come to consider the merits of views which differ from their own. Consequently, the Internet is not necessarily a medium by which new ideas and information are exchanged; it is perhaps no more than a collection of isolated cells in which individuals can "devise a communications universe of their own choosing" (2001a, 55) and hear only "louder echoes of their own voices" (2001a, 74).

Technology offers its usual lesson: technological advances are morally potent but not self-directing. New potentialities for democratic enrichment hold new possibilities for manipulation and abuse. Communications technology can help to generate an informed, engaged citizenry, but it also can erect a Tower of Babel, spread misinformation, divide, and alienate. Again, we must ask whether the triumph of democracy is simply a rhetorical triumph. That Robert Dahl should have elected in 1998 to compose a nuts-and-bolts "guide" to democracy expressly for a general readership is suggestive.

Democratic Theory in the Age of Democratic Triumph

Dahl is not alone in his concern for democracy. The casual reader browsing through the Political Science and Current Affairs sections of any reasonably stocked bookstore is bound to be struck by the titles he confronts. Democracy is "disaffected," "diminished," "unrealized," "at risk," "frustrated," "in crisis," and "on trial," among other things. Michael Sandel observes that "our public life is rife with discontent" (1996, 3); "our control over the forces that govern our lives is receding" (1982, 25), and "the moral fabric of community is unraveling around us" (1996, 2). Theda Skocpol agrees, claiming that "The great civic transformation of our time has diminished America's democracy, leaving gaping holes in the fabric of our social and political life" (2003, 254). According to Jean Bethke Elshtain, American democracy is "faltering." Describing our condition, she continues,

> We find deepening cynicism; the growth of corrosive forms of isolation, boredom, and despair; the weakening, in other words, of that world known as democratic civil society, a world of groups and associations and ties that bind. (1995, 2)

In a similar vein, Roberto Unger remarks,

> Confusion and disappointment . . . have become the common stig-
> mata of the politically conscious . . . ordinary working citizens are
> likely to feel themselves angry outsiders, part of a fragmented and
> marginalized majority, powerless to reshape the collective basis of
> the collective problems they face. They find the routes to social mo-
> bility for themselves and their children blocked in what is suppos-
> edly a classless society. They believe the people who run the country
> and its big businesses to be joined in a predatory conspiracy. They
> despair of politics and politicians, and seek an individual escape
> from a social predicament. (1998, 4)

In Ronald Beiner's words,

> We find ourselves barbarized by an empty public culture, intimi-
> dated by colossal bureaucracies, numbed into passivity by the ab-
> sence opportunities for meaningful deliberation, inflated by absurd
> habits of consumption, deflated by the Leviathans that surround us,
> and stripped of dignity by a way of living that far exceeds a human
> scale. (1992, 34)

Lawrence Cahoone claims,

> Many of the developed liberal societies of the world, and the United
> States in particular, are lurching into a future no one can foresee
> with a long list of chronic social ills to which liberalism seems to
> have no remedy. We are presented simultaneously with the impres-
> sion of unprecedented growth and power on the one hand, and in-
> curable social and economic problems on the other, a kind of
> chaotic stability. (2002, 3)

And Fareed Zakaria contends,

> [Contemporary democracy] has produced an unwieldy system, un-
> able to govern or command the respect of people. Although none
> would dare speak ill of present-day democracy, most people in-
> stinctively sense a problem. Public respect for politics and political
> systems in every advanced democracy is at an all-time low. (2003,
> 241)

From across the political spectrum comes a single refrain: Democracy
must be rethought at the most fundamental levels.

If we are to rethink democracy, we must first come to terms with how we
presently think of democracy. Here our task is clear. Modern democracy is

liberal democracy, and liberal democracy is democracy cast within a framework of social, moral, and political claims which, taken together, may be called *liberalism*. It is safe to say, with John Dryzek, that liberalism stands today as "the world's dominant political ideology" (2000, 9). The liberal underpinnings of our democratic thinking are so pervasive that we often overlook the liberal component. Indeed, today we speak of liberal democracy as simply "democracy."

Yet "times of trouble prompt us to recall the ideals by which we live" (Sandel 1996, 3). Accordingly, current political theory is fixed upon liberalism: Has it a future? What is its nature? What are the alternatives, and are any of these sufficiently comfortable to democracy?

We can say initially that contemporary liberalism is a doctrine that supplies a constraining supplement to democracy; liberalism identifies limits to place upon democratic politics. These limits are set by the liberal conception of individual rights, principles whose primary function is to protect the individual from the will of the (democratic) majority. Hence, liberalism is a political framework in which democracy operates; it is a framework that guarantees that individuals can enjoy their natural entitlement to freedom and equal treatment without interference from the state, community, or neighborhood. A direct implication of the individual liberty that liberalism secures is that citizens will disagree with each other about fundamental issues pertaining to religion, value, and goodness. Such matters are removed from the sphere of democratic politics by the liberal rights. As John Stuart Mill articulated the point, "The only freedom which deserves the name is that of pursuing our own good in our own way" (1859, 17); hence, "liberalism is about arranging institutions to allow all of us to prosper in our own individual ways" (Hardin 1999, 1).

The liberal democratic state, then, must remain neutral or impartial on matters concerning the fundamental issues over which free citizens are expected to disagree. Liberalism promotes a distinctive vision of the role of the democratic state. It is not the job of the state to promote any particular conception of "what gives value to life" (Dworkin 1978, 191), it rather serves to maintain the conditions under which liberty can flourish; in John Rawls's words, "Everyone is assured an equal liberal to pursue whatever plan of life he pleases as long as it does not violate what justice demands" (*TJ*, 81).[4] Here, justice demands simply that one does not interfere with or obstruct another's pursuits. In this sense, then, the liberal democratic state is concerned exclusively with individual citizens and their rights, and chief among these rights is the right to noninterference on matters of the good. Moreover, liberalism understands democracy as primarily a collection of procedures by which individual preferences and interests, and conflicts among them, are fairly reconciled or at least aggregated.

Critics of liberalism writing under a variety of banners, including "communitarianism," and "civic republicanism," have recently challenged the viability of a democratic politics focused solely upon individual rights and the aggregation of personal interests. On these views, democracy requires that individuals embody the virtues that make them capable of the true freedom of self-government (Hononhan 2002, 181); for freedom does not consist in noninterference, but in the ability to participate in the government of one's community (Dagger 1997, 15). Therefore, these critics insist that the state in a democratic society must go beyond liberal neutrality, it must promote a particular moral conception, it must "cultivate . . . the qualities of character necessary to the common good of self-government" (Sandel 1996, 25; cf. Maynor 2003, 206). Unlike the liberal conception of rights, which are entitlements both of and for the individual, conceived as intrinsically apart from others, the "qualities of character" and "civic virtues" promoted by the critics we are considering can be realized by individuals only in their roles as citizens (Dagger 1997, 13), and hence, only within the context of a democratic community. According to the communitarian/civic republican critique of liberalism, the democratic state must actively engage in building and sustaining proper communities; furthermore, it must aim to protect communities and their traditions, even if in some cases this involves a conflict with individual rights. Through the right kind of intervention and community support, democracy can be revitalized.

The appeal to communities and traditions evokes liberal worries regarding majority tyranny, oppression, and conformity. In response to Michael Sandel's call for a politics based on "settled roots and established traditions," Amy Gutmann has argued, "The enforcement of liberal rights, not the absence of settled community, stands between the moral majority and the contemporary equivalent of witch hunting" (1985, 319). Sandel's view that "intolerance flourishes most where forms of life are dislocated, roots unsettled, traditions undone" (1984a, 17) is naïve. His further contention that "dogmatism," "fundamentalism," and intolerance "may themselves be symptomatic reactions" to the "dislocating forces" of liberalism is implausible (1998c, 334). Gutmann's point is sound. Communities, traditions, and shared ways of life are often exclusionary, homogenizing, intolerant, and oppressive; they do not in themselves constitute fertile soil for democracy. Something must be said about the kind of community democracy requires, and many liberals share Rawls's doubt that any community can eschew the homogenizing tendencies latent within group identity (1996, 40).

However, that current antiliberal proposals for alternative understandings of democratic politics are problematic is no indication that the concerns regarding liberalism are ungrounded; that one prominent attempt to rethink democracy has failed does not entail that there is no need to re-examine liberalism. The circumstances on the international and local levels that were previously identified constitute serious blocks to democracy and must be attended to.

If we are to rethink democracy in any fruitful way, we cannot simply negate liberalism's focus on the individual and insist upon an analogous focus on the community. The tendency to engage in the either-or fallacy (namely, the fallacy of simply advocating the opposite of a view one finds faulty) must be resisted. One way to resist this tendency is to get clear on exactly where and why liberalism has gone wrong, and this requires that we directly confront liberalism in its own terms.

Therefore, I call for a conception of democracy that is not simply antiliberalism, but after liberalism. That is, we must disentangle liberalism as a series of political commitments from the various liberal theories that have been proposed as philosophical articulations and defenses of liberalism. Many of the political commitments of liberalism will be retained in some form or another, while liberal theory will be criticized and rejected. When liberal theory is rejected but the key features of liberalism retained, the result is a theory that is "liberal" in the sense that was popular in the middle of the twentieth century and represented by figures such as Bertrand Russell, Morris Cohen, and John Dewey. A liberal in this sense is a political progressive who is committed to social democracy, self-realization, some mode of economic redistribution, and the free exercise of human intelligence in confronting social problems.

Examining Liberal Theory

In the next three chapters of this study, I embark on a critical examination of some prevalent strands of liberal theory and their corresponding conceptions of democracy. I contend that liberal theory is plagued by a dilemma that cannot be adequately ameliorated within the confines of liberalism itself. I take the tradition of liberal political philosophy to consist of a series of failed attempts to allay this dilemma. The dilemma I have in mind consists in the incompatibility of two central desiderata of liberal democratic theory. On the one hand, liberalism is committed to social pluralism, diversity, and toleration of different views about the good. On the other hand, liberal democratic theorists are committed to the view that liberal democracy is normatively superior to nonliberal, nondemocratic regimes, and liberal political philosophy is directed toward establishing this normative superiority, which is often framed in terms of legitimacy. That these desiderata are at least potentially in conflict is clear. The legitimacy of liberal democracy can be established only via an appeal to the kind of normative philosophical claims about which liberal theory officially must remain neutral or impartial. When we consider the fact that liberal democracies are becoming increasingly more *socially pluralistic*, that is, home to an increasing diversity of views, lifestyles, and conceptions of the good, we find that the conflict is unavoidable.[5] Liberal theorists are faced with a dilemma: Either provide a robust normative account of the legitimacy of liberal democracy and thereby frustrate social pluralism, or accommodate social pluralism and abandon the aspiration for a cogent philosophical account of the legitimacy of democracy.

That neither offers a viable option under modern conditions should be clear. As was noted previously, there exists good reason to want some way of separating what is merely democratic rhetoric from actual democratic politics. This separation will require a robust philosophical account of what democracy is and why it is normatively superior to its imposters, such as mild oligarchy, benevolent aristocracy, or relatively liberal theocracy. On the other hand, we recognize the reality of social pluralism and the moral necessity of accommodating it. No democratic polity could be viable without allowing for a wide variety of views, voices, and lifestyles; dissent, disagreement, and difference are democracy's lifeblood (Mouffe 2000, 93; Sunstein 2003b). In other words, we see the need for both social pluralism and theory, and rightly perceive the need for a democratic vision to include both to a sufficient degree.

It is, therefore, a question of how to balance these two factors. I contend that whereas this is and always has been liberalism's problem, liberalism itself has not the resources to resolve it, and that within the context of liberal theory, the problem is strictly a dilemma. As Rainer Forst has claimed, liberal theory is "self-undermining" because it "cannot adequately explain the political-cultural presuppositions necessary for democratic community" (2002, 89). Accordingly, Chapters 2 through 4 are concerned to make the case against liberal theory as a viable philosophical framework for contemporary democratic politics. In Chapter 2, I offer an analysis of what liberalism is, and in Chapter 3, I examine the tension within liberal theory by means of discussions of key liberal theorists, including the early work of John Rawls, which has been rightly hailed as "the greatest contribution to liberal theory in our century" (Larmore 1987, 119). Then, in Chapter 4, I turn to criticisms of three recent attempts to recast the aims of liberal theory: Later Rawlsian political liberalism, William Galston's pluralist liberalism, and Richard Rorty's antifoundationalist liberalism.

This book is not solely negative in intent. The positive phase of this study most clearly gets underway in Chapter 5, where I survey some recent developments in the literature concerning deliberative democracy. I contend that whereas the deliberativist model holds the key to resolving the tension between pluralism and theory, none of the deliberativisms offered are adequate. Specifically, I argue that the various theories of deliberative democracy are too often couched in the vocabulary of either liberalism or its civic republican/communitarian rivals. Consequently, the debates surrounding deliberative democracy simply rehearse those concerning liberalism and antiliberalism. What is needed, therefore, is a fully deliberativist theory, one which is not precommitted to any particular political program.

Accordingly, in Chapter 6, I develop a proposal for a deliberativism, which draws primarily from pragmatist sources, especially the conception of inquiry promoted by Charles Peirce. Keeping an eye on the dilemma between pluralism and theory occasioned by liberalism, the deliberativism I favor proposes an epistemic conception of democracy, but at the same time, endorses a pragmatist and fallibilist epistemology, and thus can accommodate deep disagreements and differences among citizens.

Although the resulting democratic theory is not a liberal one insofar as it rejects the liberal doctrine of official state neutrality, it eschews the problems confronting communitarian and civic republican forms of antiliberalism by insisting that the formative role of the state is epistemological and not moral. More specifically, I contend that the state's formative role is that of enabling and cultivating the intellectual habits requisite to competent deliberation. Hence, the chapter concludes with a sketch of what I call the "deliberative virtues."

Of course, no deliberative theorist can claim to have had the last word about the nature and proper aims of democratic politics. This is especially the case when one proclaims to be offering a theory according to which central political decisions must be made by means of open public discourse. The deliberativism I endorse insists that all the questions remain open questions, that issues concerning the very nature of democratic deliberation and its appropriate scope are to be revisited again and again, as political circumstances require. This study closes, then, with a speculative and prospective chapter outlining some ideas concerning how we may transform existing political conditions into a more viable and dynamic democratic polity. I hope only to point a way in which further political thinking and action might develop.

Taking Pragmatism Seriously

A few preliminary clarifications are in order concerning my use of the term 'pragmatism' as a characterization of the view I shall develop. The meaning of the term 'pragmatism' has been contested since Charles Peirce first coined it at the meetings of the Metaphysical Club in Cambridge in the early 1870s. As is now well known, Peirce saw fit to renounce the term in 1905 due to what he saw as the unfortunate appropriation of the term by William James, who thought the term should be used more broadly than Peirce had used it. John Dewey, seen by many to be the culmination of the pragmatist tradition, was also critical of James's use of the term and eventually dropped the term, as well.

Despite these contestations, the term currently enjoys wide currency as the name for a number of related tendencies associated roughly with the work of Richard Rorty. Central to this current appropriation of the term are the claims that truth is not correspondence to reality because there is no world to which beliefs might correspond, that "there is no activity called 'knowing' . . ." but only "the process of justifying beliefs to audiences" (Rorty 1999, 36), and that "there is no distinction between what is useful and what is right" (Rorty 1999, 73).

As I have previously indicated, I criticize Rorty directly in Chapter 4. Here, it should be noted that my use of the term 'pragmatism' is intended to call to mind the themes and positions that figure prominently in the work of what are sometimes called the "classical" pragmatists, and in particular, the work of Charles Peirce, John Dewey, and Sidney Hook. Central to these thinkers are the claims that traditional questions of epistemology such as "Under what conditions does S know that p?"[6] should be approached in terms of how we might best inquire that philosophical theories, like all results of inquiry, must be tested via their application within experience, and, as such, are fallible and revisable in the course of further experimental inquiry, that these notions of inquiry, experience, and fallibilism are inherently social, and that there is a direct connection between proper inquiry and democratic politics.

My commitment to these claims will be most evident in the closing chapters; however, it must be emphasized that I do not aim in this book simply to clarify, explain, or comment upon the ideas of classical pragmatists. Although students of the tradition will find many familiar pragmatist themes and arguments, they will not find exegetical discussions of the works and figures of classical pragmatism. This is deliberate. I attempt in the following pages to engage in some original philosophical thinking *in a pragmatist vein*, rather than to interpret and defend some figure or text. I have tried to engage the principle nonpragmatist positions in contemporary political theory on their own terms; I have also tried to present my pragmatist position in terms that presuppose no deep sympathy for that tradition. In fact, I have made every effort to build or make explicit intellectual bridges among the positions I develop and the broader philosophical literature. In practice, this means that whenever possible, I have enlisted the work of nonpragmatist philosophers in the service of pressing my own positions. The aim is not to insist boldly that some pragmatist "got it right" and that consequently political philosophy is merely the project of realizing that figure's vision. It is rather to take the pragmatist's own fallibilism and experimentalism to heart and open new possibilities for political theory by engaging new interlocutors, asking new questions, developing new arguments, and defending new positions.

Some pragmatists will undoubtedly object to this approach. They will insist that a proper pragmatist analysis must reconstruct the vocabularies in which mainstream philosophical problems are discussed. Hence the writings of those working in the classical idiom tend to be "in house" and often addressed to a comfortable and sympathetic audience of like-minded scholars. The character of much of the recent work in pragmatism is understandable. The tradition had, for many years, been in unjustified eclipse among professional philosophers, those whose interests and research focused on the pragmatist tradition to join together for purposes of professional and moral support. Consequently, the pragmatist's virtuous aim to effect a reconstruction of traditional philosophy runs the risk of mutating into a vicious insularity according to which all proper philosophical discussion must be conducted within parameters already established by Peirce, James, or Dewey. This, in practice, leads to exclusionary habits of tacitly demanding that all philosophical interlocutors enter the pragmatist's own preferred conceptual space. Ironically, the result of this reconstructive strategy can be stagnation, dogmatism, and a monological vision of philosophical exchange.

Habits of cohesiveness and insulation that were once imposed upon those interested in classical pragmatism are no longer useful. Pragmatists today confront a new and improved professional horizon. Many factors have contributed to the mainstreaming of pragmatism, and it is not uncommon to find among analytic and continental philosophers unabashed appeals to classically pragmatist ideas, arguments, and texts. Professional academics are now prepared to re-examine the pragmatists; it is the task of contemporary pragmatists to demonstrate that such a re-examination is worthwhile. If the contemporary classical pragmatist movement has a future, it lies precisely in the process of transforming itself from an upstart insurrection against the academic status quo into a full participant in the continuing business of philosophical inquiry. The task requires more than pressing the demand that Peirce, James, Dewey, and others be taken more seriously in wider professional circles. It requires an openness on the part of pragmatists to learn from mainstream academic philosophy, to enter into the fray of current philosophical debates, to expand their philosophical vocabularies, and to develop new arguments, ideas, and proposals. The pragmatist tradition is worth reviving only to the extent that contemporary pragmatists can engage in this way. If pragmatists cannot hold their own in the ensuing exchange, they have good reason as pragmatists to abandon their doctrines. I tend to think that pragmatists can hold their own in the contemporary discussion and have something distinctive and valuable to contribute. I hope the following pages will bear this out.

CHAPTER 2

What Liberalism Is

Liberalism in Political Discourse

It is not uncommon today to hear liberalism identified with the political commitments characteristic of the Democratic party in the United States. The liberal, in this sense of the term, is one who favors social principles that emphasize the need for federal intervention to establish and maintain a just distribution of wealth, healthcare, education, and other social goods. The liberal is opposed to the conservative, who is in turn often associated with the political programs characteristic of the Republican party in the United States. Conservatism is marked by a trust in the principles of free-market economics—competition among providers of goods, individual initiative, nonintervention at the federal level, and decentralization—as sufficient means to social justice.

The conservative thus sees the liberal political program as excessive. According to the conservative, the governmental agencies and institutional apparatus necessary to secure the envisioned distribution of social goods pose a threat to freedom. Hence, Robert Nozick, an extreme conservative, has argued that the scheme of taxation necessary to fund liberal social programs is "on a par with forced labor" (1974, 169), as it "seize[s] some of a man's leisure (forced labor) for the purposes of serving the needy" (1974, 170). Nozick argues that mandatory taxation is intrusive, an unjust interference with individual liberty.

Liberals, by contrast, argue that individual liberty can be secured only under certain social conditions. For any reasonable set of individual liberties, liberals maintain that a corresponding set of political and economic conditions exist which are necessary for their exercise. Moreover, they maintain that the free market is insufficient for liberty; the conditions necessary for liberty prevail only in the presence of the kind of redistributive interventions disparaged by conservatives. A striking example of this position is developed by Henry Shue (1980), who argues for an extensive set of basic rights to healthcare, education, and financial security, on the grounds that a certain degree of health, education, and wealth is necessary for the full exercise of one's political rights. A state that does not engage in activity designed to compensate for inequalities obstructs liberty, for it fails to create and sustain conditions necessary for individual freedom.

Of course, the above contrast between liberalism and conservatism is exaggerated due to the fact that I have intentionally drawn my examples from thinkers who advance extreme versions of the general positions they represent.[1] Conservatives do not generally oppose taxation, although they are generally wary of redistributive efforts and try to minimize governmental regulation in the private sector. Likewise, liberals are not generally committed to extensive social planning and regulation, although they do tend to promote certain forms of social programming aimed towards maintaining what they consider the minimal conditions for fairness and equality. Although the more moderate forms of liberalism and conservatism tend to prevail in contemporary discourse in America, there is still room for considerable disagreement. Familiar disputes regarding the reformation of health insurance, public funding for private education in the form of vouchers, and the use of gender or race as criteria in hiring and academic admissions decisions tend to divide cleanly along the liberal/conservative dichotomy.

Liberalism Defined: Five Basic Commitments

The foregoing remarks are mostly by way of preface, for "liberalism" shall herein be employed in a way that is different from that of colloquial parlance and contemporary popular discourse. Liberalism, as the term shall here be used, denotes a distinctive collection of philosophical claims about how a state must be ordered if it is to be legitimate. Although, as we shall discover, disagreement exists among liberal theorists regarding the principal tenets of their view, Martha Nussbaum has articulated a concise statement which captures nicely the central elements of liberalism at a level of generality that can, I believe, command wide assent. Nussbaum writes,

> Liberalism holds that the flourishing of human beings taken one by one is both analytically and normatively prior to the flourishing of the state or the nation or the religious group; analytically, because

such unities do not really efface the separate reality of individual lives; normatively because the recognition of that separateness is held to be a fundamental fact for ethics, which should recognize each separate entity as an end and not as a means to the ends of others. (1997, 62)[2]

As Nussbaum's remark suggests, liberalism has as its core two powerful commitments that are related in a specific way. The first and logically primary commitment is to the *primacy of the individual*. We may define this commitment as follows:

Primacy of the Individual. *The individual person is the fundamental element of analysis in political theorizing.*

Considerable dispute exists among contemporary liberals regarding the character of this claim. For example, it can be read as the metaphysical claim that as parts are ontologically prior to wholes, so individual persons are analytically prior to social associations. Alternatively, the primacy of the individual can be construed as a prudential or practical suggestion that, for purposes of political philosophy, the individual person is to be regarded as basic.[3] In any case, however, it follows from the primacy of the individual that no social relation or association could completely contain, capture, or exhaust the nature of the individual; the individual remains always at a certain distance from its associations (Sandel 1982, 55). Despite the fact that we often identify ourselves with various social groups (religious, political, and familial), these connections to others never fully reach the ultimate nature of the self; they cannot "efface the separate reality of individual lives." For liberalism, it is the separateness of selves, not their relatedness, which is analytically primary, and thus basic to political theorizing.

Although Nussbaum does not specify the precise nature of the implication, she contends that the recognition of the primacy of the individual entails a further commitment, what we shall call *moral individualism*:

Moral Individualism. *The good of each individual is morally prior to the good of groups of individuals.*

Again, the character of this claim is widely disputed. A predominant interpretation, evoked by Nussbaum, derives from Immanuel Kant and states that as individual persons embody a special value, which Kant called "dignity" (1785, 51–52), the individual is an "end in itself," and thus can never rightly be used solely as a means to the ends of others, individually or collectively (1785, 45). Alternatively, one can advance an interpretation that eschews any such metaphysical claims about persons, as the later Rawls does when he promotes moral individualism on the basis of the "basic intuitive idea," prominent "within the tradition of democratic thought," that citizens are to be regarded as free and equal (Rawls 1985, 397). In any case, the commitment to moral individualism implies that as the purposes, aims, and objectives of social groups are subordinate to the good of the individual, the individual can never justly be required to promote a collective good. As Rawls succinctly states the idea, the individual self is "prior to the ends which are affirmed by it" (TJ, 491).[4] Of course, individuals may choose to commit their time, energy, and resources to the advancement of the good of some association such as a church or political party, and they may do so even at the expense of their own good. The point of the principle is that no one is ever *required* to do so; such commitments must be voluntarily adopted and not be the products of coercion.

Humans are creatures capable of formulating and adopting what may be called a "conception of the good." That is, our lives are informed and guided by some more or less systematic set of beliefs about what is valuable, what is worthy of pursuit, what is good, and what kind of person one should be.[5] Although this conception is subject to fluctuation and revision over time, each of us at every particular instant harbors some such conception (Rawls 1996, 12). In light of this, it is often thought to follow from the primacy of the individual and moral individualism that the project of identifying, selecting, and pursuing a conception of the good is a job properly left to the individual.[6] Presuming this implication holds, it follows that the liberal state must refrain from trying to establish and promote a particular conception of the good among its citizens. Instead, the state must indirectly promote the good of each individual by establishing and maintaining the conditions under which each may pursue his own good without undue interference. These principles are made explicit by John Stuart Mill in his *On Liberty*,

> The only freedom which deserves the name is that of pursuing our own good in our own way, so long as we do not attempt to deprive others of theirs, or impede their efforts to obtain it. Each is the proper guardian of his own health, whether bodily, or mental and spiritual. (1859, 17)

One finds a comparable expression in Kant,

> No man can compel me to be happy after his fashion . . . Instead, everybody may pursue his happiness in the manner that seems best to him, provided he does not infringe on other people's freedom to pursue similar ends . . . . (1793, 74)

And Rawls articulates a similar idea,

> [I]ndividuals find their good in different ways, and many things may be good for one person that would not be good for another . . . In a well ordered society, then, the plans of life of individuals are different in the sense that these plans give prominence to different aims, and persons are left free to determine their good . . . . (TJ, 393)

In more recent work, Rawls puts the point as follows: "Citizens as free and equal are to be at liberty to take charge of their lives," that is, they are to be at liberty to select some conception of the good and pursue it; he adds, "The only restriction on plans of life is their being compatible with the public principles of justice" (1996, 189–190).

From this view about the nature of individual liberty, a view about the purpose and scope of the state follows: "The only purpose for which power can be rightfully exercised over any member of a civilized community, against his will, is to prevent harm to others" (Mill 1859, 14). That is, state interference is justified only in cases where it is necessary to prevent one individual from obstructing another's efforts to pursue his own good. The good of the individual "is not sufficient warrant" for interference with his activity, "He cannot rightfully be compelled to do or forbear because it will be better for him to do so, because it will make him happier, because, in the opinions of others, to do so would be wise, or even right" (Mill 1859, 14). In short, "Over himself, over his own body and mind, the individual is sovereign" (Mill 1859, 14). It is the liberal state's function to protect this sovereignty against encroachment from other individuals and other states. Consequently, the liberal state itself cannot rightfully ordain and promote any particular conception of the good for individuals; its policies must be "so far as possible, independent of any particular conception of the good life, or of what gives value to life" (Dworkin 1978, 127). For in a liberal state, "Everyone is assured an equal liberty to pursue whatever plan of life he pleases as long as it does not violate what justice demands" (TJ, 81). The use of state power to enforce an official conception of the good would necessarily involve coercion, oppression, and thus, injustice. State action and policy must therefore be neutral, or impartial, with regard to different conceptions of the good life that citizens may rightfully adopt.

Hence we may derive a third commitment of liberalism, to what we shall call *moral autonomy*:

Moral Autonomy. *It is properly the prerogative of the individual to identify, select, and pursue a conception of the good.*

As this principle sets certain constraints upon the rightful scope and exercise of the coercive power of the state, we can articulate a commitment to *political noninterference*:

> **Political Noninterference.** *The state is justified in obstructing an individual in his pursuit of his conception of the good only in cases where his action interferes with another's legitimate pursuit of the good.*

The liberal's commitment to moral autonomy also constrains state action in establishing policy, hence the liberal principle of *political neutrality*:

> **Political Neutrality.** *State action and policy must be neutral among the various conceptions of the good which citizens may rightfully adopt.*[7]

Dworkin captures well these further commitments,

> Liberals believe . . . the government must be neutral in matters of personal morality . . . it must leave people free to live as they think best so long as they do not harm others. (1983, 1)

Again, these commitments are subject to various interpretations. According to a prudential reading, these further principles of liberalism simply commend good sense in light of the risks attendant on granting a state too much influence. Mill apparently has this type of account in mind when he writes that "Mankind are greater gainers by suffering each other to live as seems good to themselves, than by compelling each to live as seems good to the rest" (1859, 17).[8] Or, one may follow Kant (1793; 1788) in advancing a metaphysical interpretation; this would require a demonstration that the three further principles can be deduced from the first two.

Collectively, these five commitments capture the distinctively liberal image of how the political order should be arranged. It is the mission of the liberal political philosopher to articulate a *theory of liberalism*; that is, the liberal philosopher must determine the precise nature of these principles, construct schema according to which they may be organized and prioritized, and devise arguments in support of the principles and the proposed system of interpretation and prioritization. With an appropriately developed theory in hand, the liberal can then generate political policies in accordance with the liberal principles. Familiar accounts of basic liberal policies, such as freedom of expression, freedom of conscience, and freedom of the press, neatly fit this model. However, it should of course be emphasized that a distinction can be made between liberal policies and liberalism; one can reject liberalism as previously specified and yet endorse roughly liberal policies. That is, one may reject liberalism but accept the basic policies of liberal states.[9]

Liberalism Contrasted with Aristotelianism

We now see that the familiar differences regarding social policy discussed in the first section of this chapter are disputes occurring *within* the domain of liberal philosophy. Disputes among libertarians, socialists, and moderates of various stripes seldom concern the validity of the basic principles of liberalism, but rather how these principles are to be understood and prioritized. As liberalism tends to contain the various positions which constitute the spectrum of most popular political discussion, we may think of liberalism as an "inertial frame" (Barber 1984, 26) of political analysis; that is to say, liberalism provides the framework within which political discussion is typically conducted. As the principles of liberalism underlie most political deliberations, they are not often identified and scrutinized. To dramatize the point, liberalism is invisible because of its ubiquity.

It therefore may be instructive to examine briefly an antiliberal position. A number of important philosophers have advanced political theories which oppose the principles of liberalism, and perhaps the most notable among these is Aristotle.[10] Aristotle famously argued in the first book of his *Politics* that certain kinds of political association, such as the family, the village, and the city, or the *polis*, are not extrinsic to the nature of individuals, but logically necessary to personhood. According to Aristotle, the human being is metaphysically so constituted as to have well-being, *eudaimonia*, as its natural state of completion, *entelechia* (*NE*, 1095a15).[11] As the good, *agathos*, of each thing is identical to its completion or its aim, *telos* (*NE*, 1094a1), the good of human beings is thus well-being (*NE*, 1097b20–30). However, this good cannot be attained without proper upbringing and proper laws (*NE*, 1180a15), and these are the concerns of the *polis*, which exists "for the sake of living well" (*P*, 1252b27). Accordingly, the *polis*—and the other social institutions it implies—exists "by nature" (*P*, 1252b30), for that which is necessary to the achievement of a natural state of completion itself exists by nature and is not artificial.[12]

Aristotle therefore would not accept the primacy of the individual. Rather, he maintains, "The *polis* is by nature prior to the household and to each one of us taken singly" (*P*, 1253a18). The priority of the *polis* is, for Aristotle, a metaphysical truth; "For the whole is necessarily prior to the part" (*P*, 1253a19), and human beings are by nature parts of a *polis*—any creature that is not of a nature to require the *polis* for its completion is *ipso facto* not a man, but "either of a depraved sort or better than a human being" (*P*, 1253a1–5). Consequently, the fundamental subject matter of political philosophy is not, as liberalism holds, the individual, but rather the *polis*, its laws, and its organization.

Aristotle also rejects moral individualism. In fact, one could argue that Aristotle would find unintelligible the idea that the individual good could be separated from the good of the *polis*; according to Aristotle, the aim of the *polis* is the good for the individual (i.e., *eudaimonia*), and the individual cannot attain *eudaimonia* without the *polis*. In this sense, the individual good and the good of the *polis* are identical; however, Aristotle maintains,

> Even if the good is the same for the individual and the *polis*, the good of the *polis* clearly is the greater and more perfect thing to attain and to safeguard. The attainment of the good for one man alone is, to be sure, a source of satisfaction; yet to secure it for a nation and for *polis* is nobler and more divine. (*NE*, 1094b6–10)

Moreover, the good of the individual consists in sharing in the *polis*; an individual's good exists within his role in the *polis*. Thus, the individual's good is subordinate to that of the *polis*.

With the grounds for Aristotle's rejection of the first two liberal commitments in view, it is easy to anticipate Aristotle's reactions to the remaining liberal principles. As the *polis* exists for the sake of living well, and as it aims at this through its laws, it is clear that Aristotle would reject political neutrality; for it is the job of the *polis* to promote excellence, *arete*, in its citizens, and this requires that legislation be nonneutral among competing conceptions of the good. Any *polis* that aimed at neutrality with regard to the good would be a *polis* in name only, because it would not be performing the proper job, *ergon*, of a *polis* (*P*, 1280b29–1281a10).

Similarly, Aristotle would reject political noninterference; the reach of the *polis* extends beyond the minimal scope designated by liberal theorists. As the *polis* is not a voluntary association, but a natural association necessary to and existing for the sake of living well, its job is that of habituating its citizens to excellence. The *polis* habituates the citizens to excellence by means of its laws. However, laws alone are not sufficient for the task of promoting excellence, for these will affect only those of a "generous mind" who are already well-disposed to excellence (*NE*, 1079b7). As most people are controlled by passion rather than what is good, the *polis* must therefore employ force to secure the correct habits (*NE*, 1080a15–25). Accordingly, the influence of the *polis* extends far beyond that of the liberal state. The *polis* does not stand aloof in all but those cases in which interference is necessary to prevent one from causing harm to others. It rather plays an active and pervasive role in shaping the characters of the citizens; it is the *polis* that is to make the citizens good (Simpson 1990).

Of course, Aristotle must also reject moral autonomy. The good is not a matter of individual selection, and almost no individual can attain the good without the support of the *polis*. Again, a *polis* that leaves the pursuit of the good life up to citizens individually fails to be a *polis* in the proper sense. Persons living in such a *polis* will lack the proper habits and thus pursue a deficient conception of the good; consequently, they will live unnatural, depraved lives.

These remarks, though brief, are enough to evoke adversity in the liberal mind. To liberal ears, Aristotle's proposal sounds inherently unjust, and perhaps even dangerous. At least one liberal philosopher has gone so far as to claim that oppression and injustice are the *only* means by which one could realize Aristotle's ideal of a large group of persons embodying and sharing a single conception of the good.[13] Is Aristotle not sanctioning oppression on the order of a Stalinist, Maoist, or Medieval theocratic regime?[14] Is he not endorsing a totalitarian politics in which individuals and their lives vanish in the shadow of the omnipotent state and its needs?

Considered against the background of Aristotle's view, liberalism "offers a powerful liberating vision" (Sandel 1996, 12) of autonomy and independence. According to liberalism, each of us is at liberty to "take charge" of his own life (Rawls 1996, 189). We are not instruments of a state or of some antecedently given *telos*; we are not bound to ends and purposes set for us by nature or tradition or God. Rather, liberalism maintains that we are *agents* in the fullest sense; we are autonomous choosers of our ends and purposes, and these ends and purposes are valid simply in virtue of their being chosen by us. As Rawls would have it, individuals are "self-authenticating sources of valid claims" (1996, 32).

Moreover, liberalism provides a strong basis for social equality. Unlike Aristotle, who held that some persons were by nature subordinate to others (*P*, 1254b11–19), the liberal theorist's vision of the individual as a center of autonomous choice, a source of valid claims, renders morally irrelevant certain differences between persons. As the "self is prior to the ends which are affirmed by it" (*TJ*, 491), differences of race, religion, class, ethnicity, and gender fail to capture anything essential about individuals. Therefore, discrimination or partiality on the basis of such features is morally suspicious; for these are differences that do not, in fact, *make* a difference. According to liberalism, "Our social position and class, our sex and race should not influence deliberations made from a moral point of view" (Rawls 1975, 268). As liberal selves, we are equal.

Finally, a community based upon the liberal vision of free and equal individuals will necessarily be *tolerant* of the differences that will inevitably arise among citizens. On the liberal view, ideological, philosophical, theological, and moral differences among persons are not to be quashed or suppressed, for they are the natural outcome of "the work of free practical reason within the framework of free institutions" (Rawls 1996, 37). Indeed, deep differences among citizens regarding matters of ultimate concern are often celebrated by liberalism in the name of diversity.[15]

It is thus often said that the virtues of a liberal state are liberty, equality, and toleration. Given this, it might seem that liberalism is a political philosophy that is especially well-suited to democracy. Indeed, antiliberalism tends typically to accompany opposition to democracy, as in Plato, Aristotle, Nietzsche, Carl Schmitt, and Leo Strauss (Holmes 1993). Conversely, the tradition of liberal philosophy tends to converge with the tradition of democratic philosophy, as in John Locke, John Stuart Mill, and Isaiah Berlin. This coincidence should not be taken too strictly, however. There has recently arisen a series of formidable criticisms of liberalism that propose to show that liberalism "lacks the civil resources to sustain self-government" (Sandel 1996, 6), that liberalism and democracy do not complement each other as well as it might seem. Hence, a question central to current political theory is: Can a society based upon liberal principles generate and sustain the conditions necessary for effective democracy?

Liberalism and Antiliberalism

Opponents of liberalism fall into two classes: Those who reject democracy and those who support democracy. Examination of antidemocratic antiliberalism lies beyond the scope of our discussion. Although I shall have occasion to formulate and promote a certain conception of democracy in the coming chapters, the legitimacy of democracy is presupposed. We therefore shall focus upon democratic antiliberalism.

It is unfortunate that academic debate concerning liberalism has been named the "liberal-communitarian debate"; for it is conceded that this title is unsatisfactory as it understates the variety of views at work in the dispute.[16] For our purposes, it is necessary to distinguish two varieties of democratic antiliberalism, which are sometimes run together under the name "communitarianism." I distinguish "communitarianism" from "civic republicanism."

The communitarian variety of democratic antiliberalism is composed mostly of sociologists, political scientists, and politicians concerned with the disturbing trends of isolation, nonparticipation, and apathy in liberal societies, especially the United States.[17] Communitarians advance proposals for repairing a fragmented public sphere; they tend to be politically active, advocating political legislation that is designed to restore community, cooperation, and a sense of belonging among citizens.[18]

Civic republicanism, by contrast, tends to focus upon the theoretical underpinnings of liberalism. Civic republicans particularly criticize liberalism's emphasis upon negative liberty, insisting that freedom does not consist in the absence of interference, but rather in the positive capacity to be self-governing (Sandel 1996, 5) and not subject to domination (Pettit 1997). Civic republican freedom thus requires the rejection of the familiar liberal commitment to state neutrality; to realize true freedom, the state must undertake the formative project of cultivating in citizens the "qualities of character that self-government requires" (Sandel 1996, 6).

Very often, however, civic republicans remain at the theoretical level of analysis, leaving questions of actual policy to the side; it is "one thing to criticize liberalism as a philosophical theory and quite another thing to engage in conflict with contemporary liberal politics" (MacIntyre 1998, 244). Indeed, liberals often wonder what the theoretical differences between liberals and republicans amount to in the practical realm of social policy. Will Kymlicka, for example, has characterized the debate between left-leaning liberals, like himself, and left-leaning civic republicans, such as Sandel, as "internecine, unnecessary, and counterproductive":

> People on the left who agree on 95 percent of the actual issues confronting our society spend all of their time arguing with each other about the five percent of issues we disagree about, rather than fighting alongside each other for the 95 percent of issues we have in common. (Kymlicka 1998, 134)

The perceived similarity on issues of policy have led liberals to conceive of civic republicanism as a corrective to liberal politics, a way of avoiding the excesses to which liberalism may tend, but not strictly an alternative theory. "The worthy challenge" posed by civic republicanism "is not to replace liberal justice, but to improve it" (Gutmann 1985, 322).[19]

It is therefore tempting to cast the distinction I am pressing between communitarians and civic republicans as a difference between the main focus of their respective critiques of liberalism. One could argue with some justification that communitarians target perceived defects in liberal society and liberal policy whereas civic republicans aim to undermine liberal theory. This way of construing the distinction is generally helpful, but it should not suggest that the communitarian and civic republican projects are strictly exclusive; as indicated previously, these distinct varieties of democratic antiliberalism sometimes run together. The policies endorsed by communitarians are sometimes shared by those espousing a civic republican political philosophy. Moreover, communitarians are typically driven to address the philosophical foundations of liberalism, and are often found advancing civic republican arguments. Again, the streams diverge; many civic republicans explicitly distance themselves from communitarianism, and some derive roughly liberal policies from civic republican theory.[20]

It is more useful to characterize the distinction between communitarians and civic republicans as a difference regarding the relation between theory and practice, or, to cast the distinction another way, between philosophy and politics. Communitarians tend to begin with troubling social phenomena; they then typically contrive policies which they surmise will improve the current state of affairs, and formulate a theoretical basis for their proposals ad hoc. The result is often a sweeping and comprehensive vision of society rich with policy proposals, but weak on theory, and consequently vulnerable to misinterpretation and obvious objections.

Amitai Etzioni provides a clear example of these tendencies. Etzioni begins a recent book outlining the essentials of his communitarian politics with the identification of some important social ills: "The deterioration of private and public morality, the decline of the family, high crime rates, and the swelling of corruption in government" (1993, 2). He then offers as his diagnosis the "self-centered, me-istic orientations" (1993, 24) prevalent in contemporary society. He proposes that society is "suffering from a severe case of deficient we-ness and the values that only communities can properly uphold"; consequently, "restoring communities and their moral voices [is] what our current conditions require" (1993, 26). He advises us to "return to the language of social virtue" (1993, 7), and to "raise our moral voice a decibel or two" (1993, 36) in order to "shore up our moral foundations" (1993, 11).

What Etzioni does not make explicit is *how* following these prescriptions will result in lower crime rates, less corruption, more cooperation, and stronger families; he fails to do the theoretical work of showing how restoring communities will solve social problems. With this work undone, Etzioni is open to the objection that his apotheosized "we-ness" is a recipe for a more intolerant, oppressive, and unjust society. With the community understood as the source and repository of the moral values that we are supposed to "shore up" and "transmit" (1993, 12), we run the familiar risk of majority tyranny. Certainly, the prevailing moral voice of the community will simply be the voice of the majority, and history has unfortunately done us the service of providing many compelling proofs that majorities are capable of sanctioning and perpetrating acts of severe evil.

When he is forced to confront this objection, Etzioni finds himself without the theoretical resources necessary for a plausible reply. Despite the fact that he has placed the source of morality within the community, he must also maintain that there are certain "higher-order values," which "no community has a right to violate" (1993, 37). We discover in Etzioni's recent writings that these "overarching values" are identified in the Bill of Rights, and the liberties and protections specified there are "exempt from majority rule" (1995, 23). Of course, this appeal does not answer the objection, it simply delays it. If Etzioni is asked, "What is the *justification* for the 'higher-order values' specified in the Bill of Rights?" he must either appeal to majority consensus or to some other source of legitimacy. If he appeals to majority consensus, he has not responded to the objection; if he identifies some other source of legitimacy, he will have to admit some community-independent source of valid moral principles.[21] If he admits a community-independent source of valid moral principles, he will have thereby surrendered an essential feature of his communitarianism.

Civic republicans, by contrast, tend to place theory prior to practice. Maintaining that "to engage in a political practice is already to stand in relation to theory" (Sandel 1984b, 12), civic republicans see the defects of liberal politics as the outcome of a deficient theory. This is not to say that all citizens harbor a philosophical theory of society in their daily lives, nor is it to say that liberal political philosophers have persuaded citizens of contemporary democracies to adopt a liberal political theory.[22] It is rather to say that our political practice is informed by a specific, though perhaps tacit, theory that is implicit in our practice; liberalism provides the theoretical and conceptual vocabulary by means of which current democratic politics gets done, it "sets the terms of political discourse and describes the self-understandings implicit in our political and constitutional practices" (Sandel 1998c, 320).

Civic republicans seek to address liberalism as a philosophical theory and eventually to replace it with an alternate theory they believe more congenial to healthy democratic politics. To the charge that civic republican political philosophy is insufficiently suggestive of specific policies, civic republicans may reply that once the conditions requisite for a flourishing and self-governing polity are in place, the policy decisions should be left to democratic processes. Such a response certainly affirms the envisioned relationship between political theory and practice; however, it also leaves open the question of whether civic republican politics can, in practice, avoid the troubling policy implications associated with communitarianism.

A Test Case: Pornography and Obscenity

The distinctions I have identified among liberal, communitarian, and civic republican political philosophy may be further illuminated by means of a brief examination of a particular social question that has exercised liberal and antiliberal thinkers alike. The cluster of questions concerning the proper stance of a democratic society toward pornography and modes of offensive expression provides a convenient position from which to launch an exploration of the different styles of political analysis. As the objective of such an examination is not to compare the policies endorsed by the theorists to be discussed, but rather to illustrate the differences in analytical approach, I shall focus attention upon the different ways in which the theorists frame the *question* regarding pornography.

Given the commitment to political noninterference, liberal discussions concerning legal bans on pornographic material tend to focus upon questions regarding the competing rights involved. On the one hand, pornography seems to be protected by the First Amendment, which disallows the abridgement of free speech. On the other hand, some argue that pornography is causally linked to acts of violence against women and to the existence of socially pervasive attitudes about women and sexuality which promote practices that are unfair to women; pornography, it is alleged, therefore constitutes a violation of the civil rights of women. The relevant questions for the liberal, then, are: (1) Does the production and distribution of pornography constitute a violation of anyone's rights?; and (2) Does the prohibition of pornography constitute a violation of anyone's rights? As the First Amendment provides a *prima facie* case for answering the second question affirmatively, the liberal who would support a ban on pornography must show that the harm of pornography is sufficiently extreme as to override the pornographer's rights to expression.

The liberal mode of political analysis is exhibited clearly in a round of debates concerning a controversial amendment proposed to the Minneapolis Civil Rights Ordinance in 1983—later proposed in 1984 to the City Council of Indianapolis—claiming that pornography "is a form of discrimination on the basis of sex" and thus should be subject to extensive legal regulation.[23] In support of the ordinance, Catherine MacKinnon argues, "The harm of pornography, broadly speaking, is the harm of the civil inequality of the sexes made invisible as harm because it has become accepted as the sex difference" (1987, 63). Supporting MacKinnon's position, Rae Langton writes,

> Women are apparently disadvantaged by the permissive policy [regarding pornography], and therefore have a *prima facie* cause for complaint. Some women feel deeply distressed and insulted by it, and it is probable that the existence of such pornography reinforces and perpetuates attitudes and beliefs that undermine the well-being of women and undermines sexual equality; it probably contributes, for example, to an environment in which sexual abuse is more likely to occur. (1990, 106–107)

Maintaining that the proposed ordinance is unconstitutional, Ronald Dworkin argues,

> Lawyers who defend the Indianapolis ordinance argue that society does have a further justification for outlawing pornography: It causes great harm, as well as offense, to women. But their arguments mix together claims about different kinds of harm, and it is necessary to distinguish these. They argue, first, that some forms of pornography significantly increase the danger that women will be

raped or physically assaulted. If that were true, and the danger were clear and present, then it would indeed justify censorship of those forms . . . . In fact, however, although some evidence exists that exposure to pornography weakens people's critical attitudes towards sexual violence, no persuasive evidence exists that it causes more actual incidents of assault. (1993a, 117)

In each case, one finds that the relevant consideration in determining the status of a prohibition on the production and distribution of pornography is the degree to which pornography constitutes harm. Those who support antipornography legislation argue that pornography does harm women and in a way sufficient to warrant legal prohibition. Those who reject antipornography legislation deny that pornography harms sufficiently to require special action. This is not to say, however, that those who support the rights of pornographers and consumers of pornographic material believe that pornography is morally unproblematic. On a liberal analysis, the question of the moral value of pornography is irrelevant. For the liberal, the issue turns not upon the moral effects of exposure to pornography on the characters of those who consume it, or the morality of participation in the industry that produces pornography; the liberal's commitment to the principle of neutrality requires that policies are, insofar as possible, neutral with regard to questions of the good. The determining consideration is simply whether the production and distribution of pornography violates anyone's rights.

Communitarians, such as Etzioni, take a different approach. Noting the "gap between rights and rightness" (Galston 1991, 8), communitarians maintain that the legal right to free expression does not entail the moral rightness of every instance of free expression. Arguing that antiobscenity laws treat symptoms rather than the disease, Etzioni offers a nonlegal (1993, 200–201) analysis of questions concerning questionable modes of expression which relies less upon the coercive apparatus of the state and more upon "community-based mechanisms" (1996, 29) of approval and disapproval. In a passage relating particularly to obscene speech, Etzioni writes,

> While respecting the legal right of individuals to engage in obscene and inflammatory speech, a community is fully entitled, in effect called upon, to inform those who spout venom that it is deeply offended by their speech. Members of the community are well within their rights when they seek to dissociate themselves from people who speak that way. (1995, 30)

As this quotation indicates, the relevant question for Etzioni is not whether antipornography legislation would violate the rights of those who produce and consume it; rather, he is concerned to articulate a strategy for dealing with what he considers an obvious social evil. Apparently, we as a community should recognize rights to free expression, even in cases of obscenity, but undertake community action designed to encourage pornographers and others who choose to engage in acts of obscene expression to "put their First Amendment rights to better use" (1993, 204).

The philosophical difficulties that this proposal invites need not concern us at this point. Instead, it is important to note that Etzioni's concerns are strictly practical. He shows no doubt that pornography and other forms of offensive expression are bad for society and that curbing offensive expression would be a positive good. Moreover, Etzioni rejects attempts to control obscenity by legal means, not because of any special dedication to the First Amendment, but rather because he is convinced that such legal measures are bound to fail. The solution, again, lies within the "moral voice" of the community (1993, 7).

Civic republicans such as Sandel pose the question regarding pornography in a way that differs from that of both the liberal and the communitarian. Whereas the liberal is strictly concerned with upholding and protecting individual rights, and the communitarian seeks to empower the community's moral voice, the civic republican rejects both approaches, maintaining that the question regarding the legality of pornography turns upon the *moral* character of the practices in question.

We may begin with Sandel's rejection of the communitarian approach. As our examination of Etzioni's analysis contends, the communitarian opposes pornography on the grounds that such expression offends the community's values. According to Etzioni, the problem regarding obscenity is generated by the weakening of the moral voice of the community. The appropriate response, then, is that of reasserting the community's values through community action designed to express group disapproval. Civic republicans reject the majoritarianism implicit in the communitarian analysis and strategy. On the civic republican view, there is nothing sacrosanct about the moral standards and shared understandings of a given community as such. "The mere fact that certain practices are sanctioned by the traditions of a particular community is not enough to make them just" (Sandel 1998b, xi). What is missing from the communitarian analysis is a mechanism by which the community's shared values may be evaluated; the civic republicans demand an "independent, external standard that sheds light on whether identity-constituting communities confer worth upon their members beyond the bare fact of possessing something shared" (Beiner 1992, 29).

The civic republican response to the liberal analysis is more nuanced. As was indicated in our examination above, the liberals' commitment to political neutrality requires that their deliberations concerning the legality of pornography and other forms of offensive expression cannot presume, favor, privilege, or disallow any particular conception of the good life that citizens may rightfully adopt. The liberals aspire to neutrality in their policies, and therefore, propose to leave aside questions about the good for purposes of public deliberation. This aspiration may be characterized as that of placing the right prior to the good, as it attempts to derive a conception of justice from premises which make no reference to any particular conception of the human good.

Sandel rejects the liberal conception of the relation of the right to the good. He denies that the principles of justice can be derived independently of any consideration of the human good.[24] According to the civic republican view,

> . . . principles of justice depend for their justification on the moral worth or intrinsic good of the ends they serve . . . the case of recognizing a right depends on showing that it honors or advances some important human good. (Sandel 1998b, xi)

The question concerning the legality of offensive forms of expression turns upon a moral judgment regarding the content of the expression. For civic republicans like Sandel, this moral judgment rests upon a conception of the character traits citizens must embody if they are to be competent participants in a self-governing community of citizens. The question, then, is not whether pornography violates individual rights, but rather, does free expression in cases of pornography serve human ends that are sufficiently good and important to warrant protection? Sandel does not offer a decisive response to this question, for his civic republicanism is not offered as an instrument for advocating certain policies, but rather as an alternative framework of political philosophy, one which recognizes the dangers of divorcing political theorizing and political discourse from "substantive engagement" with controversial "moral and cultural" questions (Sandel 1998c, 329).[25]

By means of these contrasts, we have further clarified the distinctions I have drawn between the liberal, communitarian, and civic republican modes of political theorizing. The liberal approach involves an analysis of competing rights claims and a bracketing off of questions about the good. The communitarian approach subordinates concerns about individual rights to those of the communal good, but does so in a way that places the community's moral voice beyond moral evaluation. Likewise, the civic republican approach places the good prior to the right but replaces the majoritarianism of the communitarians for a stance that may be characterized as "teleological" or "perfectionist" (Sandel 1998b, xi). That is, civic republicans attack the liberal strategy of trying to derive principles of justice independently of considerations of the good. They instead argue for a conception of justice and a political theory that attends especially to the kind of questions that liberalism seeks to ignore. Of course, liberals worry that the perfectionism of civic republicanism holds little advantage in practice over the communitarians' majoritarianism. Liberals argue that the civic republican's conception of virtue will be merely a philosophical elaboration of the attitudes and prejudices prevailing in a given community. It is not clear that the civil republicans can offer a convincing response to this challenge. As the positive proposal I shall offer in the second part of this book draws from civic republican ideas, we shall have occasion to revisit this question later.

CHAPTER 3
Tension in Liberal Theory

In the preceding chapter, I identified five fundamental commitments that constitute liberalism as an inertial frame of political analysis. They are as follows:

1. **Primacy of the Individual.** The individual person is the fundamental element of analysis in political theorizing.
2. **Moral Individualism.** The good of each individual is morally prior to the good of groups of individuals.
3. **Moral Autonomy.** It is properly the prerogative of the individual to identify, select, and pursue a conception of the good.
4. **Political Noninterference.** The state is justified in obstructing an individual in his pursuit of his conception of the good only in cases where his action interferes with another's legitimate pursuit of the good.
5. **Political Neutrality.** State action and policy must be neutral among the various conceptions of the good that citizens may rightfully adopt.

Drawing on these commitments, we can roughly define liberalism. It is the view according to which the political order is legitimate when the individual is taken to be both analytically and normatively primary. This primacy acknowledges that each individual is moral, autonomous, and can choose his or her own ends and values, and this autonomy acknowledges serious constraints on the action of political entities (such that they must maintain a posture of noninterference except in well-defined circumstances, and thus must also maintain an official policy of moral neutrality in deciding policy and adjudicating disputes among individuals).

Liberalism, as a normative vision of politics, is distinct from the various attempts to construct a compelling liberal theory. *Theories* of liberalism are attempts to articulate liberalism precisely and to defend the liberal political order philosophically. Several distinct varieties of liberal theory are presently in currency; although some of these are clearly more viable than others, I shall not in this chapter be concerned to compare the merits of the major liberal theories relative to their liberal competitors. Instead, I aim to develop a critique of the project of liberal theory; more specifically, I shall argue that the very idea of a liberal theory contains a tension that cannot be resolved. In this chapter, I demonstrate this tension mainly by means of an analysis of the extremely influential liberal theory articulated by Rawls in *A Theory of Justice*. Before turning to this, however, some stage setting of a more general sort is required.

Aspirations of Traditional Liberal Theory

Traditional liberal theory is marked by a trio of related justificatory aspirations. The first of these may be called the *philosophical* aspiration of liberal theory. Liberal thinkers proposed philosophical principles from which the legitimacy of a liberal political order could be derived. In this sense, traditional theorists of liberalism presupposed a foundationalist view of political justification; they thought that the liberal political order was in need of philosophical support and that the legitimacy of the liberal regime depended upon philosophical premises. Hence, one finds in Locke (1689a) appeals to divinely conferred rights as the foundation from which a liberal politics follows. In Kant (1785), it is the very idea of rational agency that provides the groundwork for the liberal state. Mill's liberalism (1859) follows from the combination of hedonism with the Greatest Happiness Principle. In the philosophical tradition, the project of identifying theoretical foundations for liberal politics was taken as the distinctive office of liberal philosophy. The aim of liberal philosophy, then, was to devise a firm philosophical foundation for liberalism.

The remaining two aspirations concern the scope of liberal theory's philosophical ground. Since liberalism entails that the consent of those subject to any proposed political order is a necessary condition for the legitimacy of that order, liberal thinkers of the past aimed for a theory that could, in principle, command the assent of all persons subject to the liberal state. Call the aspiration for an account of liberalism that can command the assent of all liberal citizens, the *consensus* aspiration.

The aspiration for consensus places some constraints upon the kind of philosophical claim to which one may appeal in constructing the groundwork for the liberal state. These constraints have generated the familiar liberal dichotomies between the right and the good on the one hand, and the public and the private on the other. It was thought that, although citizens may never reach consensus concerning the good life, they may be brought to agree upon a set of uncontestable first principles which could establish the general public framework within which each may peruse his own private ends. Insisting that political first principles could be derived independently of the theory of the good, questions of the good were relegated to the private realm, and liberal theory was focused almost exclusively upon the theory of the right.

A philosophical ground for liberal politics that aspires to win the assent of citizens who may be divided at the level of the good must appeal to some purportedly fundamental fact about human beings or to some commonality that underlies the differences among individual persons. Traditionally, the idea of a universal human nature is employed to this end. If, as Kant argued (1785), it is the very nature of a human being to be an autonomous agent, one can devise a theory of the right drawing only upon considerations regarding the conditions necessary for autonomous agency. Alternatively, if Jefferson (1776) is correct to assert that every individual is created equal, then this fundamental equality can serve as a basis for politics. Kantian autonomy and Jeffersonian equality may be asserted without invoking or favoring any specific conception of the good; hence, they may be the focus of a consensus among citizens otherwise divided over moral and religious fundamentals.

However, if the philosophical foundation for liberalism is sought within purportedly universal facts about human beings, then the resulting theory will serve not only to legitimize the liberal state, it will also serve to demonstrate the illegitimacy of antiliberal regimes. In this way, the traditional liberal theorists aspired to produce a universally valid political philosophy, according to which of all possible regimes, only a liberal regime is legitimate. Hence, the traditional theories are addressed not merely to some local population of liberal citizens, but ultimately to humans as such. Call the aspiration for a universally valid account the *universalist* aspiration of liberal theory.

Thus, despite the important differences among liberal theories in their analyses of the precise nature of the characteristically liberal commitments, all traditional liberal theories accept the same view of political justification.[1] Specifically, the traditional theories share the view that liberalism must be justified by means of appeal to some more general philosophical theory. Liberalism is therefore not entirely separate from the presupposed background theory; the success of the proposed liberal theory will depend in part upon the strength of the background theory upon which it rests. If a proposed theory of liberalism finds its ground in a suspect or false background theory, exposing the background view will constitute a suitable challenge to the liberal theory in question.

Keeping with the current nomenclature, we may describe a liberal theory as comprehensive when it attempts to ground liberalism in a philosophical theory; accordingly, theorists offering comprehensive theories will be called "comprehensive liberals."[2] The comprehensive liberal is to be contrasted with the "noncomprehensive liberal." Unlike the comprehensive liberal, who takes liberalism to rest upon or follow from a philosophical doctrine, the noncomprehensive liberal takes liberalism to be, in Rawls's words, "freestanding" (1989, 474; 1996, 10). That is, a liberal theory that is noncomprehensive "offers no specific metaphysical or epistemological doctrine beyond what is implied by the political conception itself" (Rawls 1996, 10); it "stays on the surface, philosophically speaking," seeking to "leave aside philosophical controversies whenever possible," and to "avoid philosophy's long-standing problems" (Rawls 1985, 395). In Rawls's own noncomprehensive theory, which is called "political liberalism," liberal theorists should not attempt to devise a robust philosophical proof of liberalism from some fundamental theory; rather, they must begin "from within a certain political tradition" drawing "solely upon basic intuitive ideas" that are "embedded in the political institutions" of that tradition (Rawls 1985, 390). Rorty has made the point succinctly: The noncomprehensive liberal "puts democratic politics first, and philosophy second" (1988, 191). Two leading varieties of noncomprehensive theory will be critically examined in the next chapter. At present, our focus shall be comprehensive liberal theory.

The Tension Defined: Liberalism and Social Pluralism

A difficulty with the justificatory aspirations of comprehensive liberal theories arises once we note that liberal societies generate *social pluralism*. That is, in any society marked by the individual liberties and protections specified by the liberal principles, one should expect to find among citizens a number of distinct visions of the good life, value, obligation, purpose, and human nature. These visions will often be incompatible with each other; consequently, conflicts between them will be difficult to resolve in ways that are acceptable to the conflicted parties. Thus, reconciliation and deep moral unity is not likely to be forthcoming; social pluralism is here to stay. Furthermore, this openness to a wide diversity of lifestyles, moral and religious visions, and philosophical temperaments is often regarded as a principal normative advantage of liberalism; as Mill says, the freedom "of pursuing our own good in our own way" is the only freedom "which deserves the name" (1859, 17). On the liberal view, then, a properly ordered society is necessarily a socially pluralistic society. In fact, Rawls has gone as far as to claim that the absence of social pluralism is a clear symptom of oppression; he writes, "a continuing shared understanding on one comprehensive religious, moral, or philosophical doctrine can be maintained only by the oppressive use of state power" (1996, 37).

I take the claim that the liberal political order generates social pluralism to be descriptive and noncontroversial. Of course, philosophers have offered various theories of social pluralism. Epistemological accounts hold that since human reason is imperfect and questions of ultimate value are highly complex, one cannot expect all competent reasoners to come to agreement on matters of philosophical, moral, and religious fundamentals. Another strand of theory understands social pluralism as primarily the outcome of certain facts about the ontology of value. On this kind of view, the facts about values are themselves "plural" in that incompatible statements, each of which prescribes different actions and judgments, may be true at the same time.

I need not enter into the debates concerning these different philosophical accounts here; they will be addressed somewhat in the next chapter. The point is that social pluralism, no matter how it is understood, tends to frustrate the aspirations of comprehensive liberal theory (Gray 2000a; 2000b). If there are no fundamental premises that all rational humans share, or can be rationally persuaded to share, then there is no raw material from which a universally valid philosophical account of liberalism can be constructed. Similarly, where the citizens of a given society are deeply divided at fundamental levels, there can be no single philosophical argument for a liberal polity that can command the assent of all rational citizens. Put another way, whereas liberalism is committed to a set of formal principles that place the individual's liberty to pursue "his own good in his own way," the liberal theorist aspires to provide a philosophical account of liberalism that will establish the universal legitimacy of the liberal political order. Such an account, if it is to be successful, must appeal to premises that can, in principle, win the assent of all. Yet social pluralism, in part, entails that that there are no such premises. Thus, the theoretical aspirations of liberal theory are in conflict with the content of the liberal political principles; liberal theory is inconsistent with the pluralism that is the result of liberal practice. Hence the tension.

The tradition of liberal theory may be read as a series of attempts to negotiate this tension. As Rawls, in *A Theory of Justice*, places himself squarely within this tradition, it may be helpful to briefly consider the trajectory of liberal theory running from Locke through Kant and Mill. What we shall find is that this historical progression is marked by an increasing deflation of the proposed philosophical groundwork of liberalism from theology, to metaphysics, and finally to psychology.

Locke's contractarianism begins from the ambitious claim that individuals are logically basic to political theorizing due to certain theological truths. As God has created individuals to be "equal and independent" (1689a, sec. 6), no individual is rightfully subordinate to another or any group of others (hence the equality), and no individual is defined by his relations to others (hence the independence); thus individuals are endowed with divinely-conferred natural rights to life, liberty, and property. Social associations—and thus social institutions, such as a state—are artificial insofar as they are, when just, generated from a contract on the part of individuals to "mutually enter into one community, and make one body politic" (1689a, sec. 14). On Locke's view, a contract among equal and independent bearers of natural rights gives rise to a liberal political order, and no other order is consistent with the idea of such a contract.

Of course, there is much more to say about Locke's theory; however, his justificatory apparatus is evident. Liberalism is underwritten by a theological doctrine of natural rights. Difficulties arise for this account once it is acknowledged that the proposed theological truths, which constitute its foundation, are contestable, and, contrary to what Jefferson may have thought, not self-evident. What can theological liberalism say to a nonbeliever, or to one who believes in a God that is not a Creator? As Locke claims in his *Letter Concerning Toleration*, "The taking away of God, though but even in thought, dissolves all"; he hence argues that "those are not at all to be tolerated who deny the being of a God. Promises, covenants, and oaths, which are the bonds of human society, can have no hold upon an atheist" (1689b, 313). Although the theological foundation for liberalism is philosophically sturdy, the resulting liberal theory is insufficiently pluralistic.

Theological claims are inappropriate for grounding a political order among whose central entailments are that individuals must be free to decide for themselves their theological commitments. Perhaps then, theology could be left to the side and a purely metaphysical case for liberalism developed? Such a case would avoid claims about the divine origin of man's rights. A metaphysical theory would instead argue that the principles of liberalism follow from certain metaphysical truths about individuals. The classic source of such a view is Immanuel Kant.

Kant's liberalism begins from the Enlightenment observation that whereas "everything in nature works according to laws," only a *rational* being has the "capacity to act according to the conception of laws (i.e., according to principles)" (1785, 29). It is precisely our ability to reason that makes humans capable of freedom. We are not simply creatures of inclination, habit, and instinct, we are creatures capable of *autonomy*, of acknowledging universal moral principles and acting on them simply *because* they are universal moral principles. Insofar as our actions are determined by reason and not by an empirical contingency or external force, we are autonomous and, therefore, free. Freedom, in both the metaphysical and political senses, consists in the ability to be the rational source and author of one's actions, to be unhindered by external influence, to be uncoerced. The liberal order, then, is the only legitimate political arrangement because it is the only one that can properly recognize and respect individual autonomy:

> A constitution allowing the greatest possible human freedom in accordance with laws which ensure that the freedom of each can coexist with the freedom of all *the others* (not one designed to provide the greatest possible happiness, as this will, in any case, follow automatically), is at all events a necessary idea which must be made the basis not only of the first outline of a political constitution but of all laws as well. (Kant 1781, 191)

There are many problems to be raised with Kant's liberal theory. Chief among these for our purposes is that Kant's metaphysical argument proves too strong. As Robert Paul Wolff (1998) has demonstrated, a Kantian view of autonomy renders all workable political arrangements illegitimate.[3] Wolff's argument can be stated easily: Individual autonomy is inviolable. When an autonomous agent acts, he does so because he has found that his action accords with a categorically valid moral principle. The autonomous agent, therefore, never obeys the commands of another.[4] Autonomous agency is thus incompatible with obedience. Now, if we understand the state to be a body endowed with the power to coerce individuals to comply with its laws,[5] the following difficulty arises: If it is the principal obligation of the individual to refuse to be obedient, and if it is the primary role of the state to use force, or the threat of force, to win obedience, then there could be no such thing as a legitimate or *de jure* state. The autonomy of the individual is incompatible with the legitimate authority of the state (1998, 18).[6]

If we base liberalism in a metaphysics that maintains on *a priori* grounds that the individual is an essentially autonomous bearer of inviolable negative rights, we shall have difficulty accounting for political authority. This problem is not simply formal. As communitarian and civic republican critics of this style of liberal theory have argued, the conflict between autonomy and authority renders liberalism unable to give a coherent account of the importance of citizenship. Thus Benjamin Barber identifies an anarchistic "disposition" within liberalism.[7] According to Barber, the liberal emphasis upon an "absolutist conception of individual rights" inhibits sociality, dilutes the constitutive bonds between persons, and engenders hostility to political power. Hence, liberalism involves a disposition toward "antipolitics" (1984, 6), and constitutes an "obstacle" to a "strong," participatory democracy (1984, 11).

Perhaps the proper response is to abandon the metaphysical project and develop liberalism from ordinary empirical considerations about persons. Such a theory would, of course, have none of the necessity and *a priori* force of a strictly metaphysical theory, but it would perhaps avoid the predicament of incompatible political commitments. We turn to the classic utilitarianism of Jeremy Bentham and John Stuart Mill for such a theory.

Utilitarians begin their analysis with the claim that the only objects of intrinsic value are certain psychological states. Specifically, the utilitarian maintains that pleasure is intrinsically good and pain is intrinsically bad; all other goods are good insofar as they produce pleasure and prevent or mitigate pain.[8] This thesis concerning value, which is called *hedonism*, is intended to be a strictly empirical, psychological fact about humans. The utilitarian next argues that an action is right in the degree to which it maximizes that which is of intrinsic value.[9] Since happiness is good, and unhappiness bad, wherever and to whomever it occurs, one ought to act so as to bring about the greatest balance of pleasure over pain for as many persons as possible. The point is intuitive: More good in the world is better than less good; thus right action thus consists of producing as much good as one's circumstances allow.

The utilitarian next asserts that what holds for individual action holds also for public policy and the official actions of governments and legislators.[10] The action of an individual agent is right in the degree to which it maximizes general happiness; similarly, the action of a state in the form of law or policy is legitimate in the degree to which it promotes or sustains the happiness of every individual it affects.

Such is the groundwork of utilitarian liberalism in its classical formulation. The utilitarian argument for liberalism, which is most forcefully presented in Mill's *On Liberty* (1859), is that liberalism maximizes individual happiness. The argument is clear: Since the individual is the best judge of what brings him pleasure, he is most likely to achieve happiness under conditions in which he can freely choose his own way of life. Thus, the best political arrangement is the one that maximizes the opportunity of the individual to discover the way of life that suits him best. Mill writes, "Mankind are greater gainers by suffering each other to live as seems good to themselves, than by compelling each to live as seems good to the rest" (1859, 17).

Of course, Mill recognizes that the freedom of each individual to live as he thinks best cannot be unconditional. What can be said to the person who decides that a life of tyrannizing others is best for him? Since it is the concern of the state to maximize general happiness, there must be certain constraints placed upon individuals with regard to the ways of living they may elect to practice. That is, each individual is to be as free as is consistent with an equal degree of liberty for every other individual. Thus Mill's "harm principle" is as follows:

> The sole end for which mankind [is] warranted, individually or collectively, in interfering with the liberty of action of any of their number, is self-protection. That the only purpose for which power can be rightfully exercised over any member of a civilized community, against his will, is to prevent harm to others. (1859, 14)

A standard objection to utilitarian theories of liberalism is that they cannot countenance a sufficiently strong theory of individual rights. Political rights will always be viewed by the utilitarian as empirical generalizations concerning the best means of maximizing general happiness.[11] Accordingly, individual rights will always be contingent upon considerations about how best to maximize the good in society. The utilitarian, therefore, can provide *no necessary* justification of liberalism, no strictly deductive proof of the liberal principles. Rather, the justification of liberalism is always contingent upon actual political conditions and how they might be manipulated to maximize the good. Could it be shown that happiness would be maximized by instituting theocratic rule or slavery, the utilitarian would have to renounce liberalism altogether? Since individual rights are, for the utilitarian, means to the maximization of the good, consistency demands that the utilitarian admit that, at least under certain conditions, the institution of slavery would be permissible and even right. The utilitarian cannot therefore maintain that slavery is *necessarily* or *intrinsically* unjust.

It is often argued by utilitarians that the doctrine leads to illiberal practices only under extremely rare counterfactual conditions. However, consider the actual policies Mill endorses in his *Considerations on Representative Government*. There, Mill is forced to reckon with issues regarding the value of democratic processes for maximizing the general good. There is good reason to think that democratic arrangements will, in fact, *not* tend to maximize general happiness. Mill thus admits,

> No one but a fool . . . feels offended by the acknowledgment that there are others whose opinion, and even whose wish, is entitled to a greater amount of consideration than his. (1861b, 335)

Mill then attempts to give this principle institutional force in the democratic process,

> The only thing which can justify reckoning one person's opinion as
> equivalent to more than one is individual mental superiority; and
> what is wanted is some approximate means of ascertaining that.
> (1861b, 336)

Mill suggests that those who are well-educated ("graduates of universities") and that are employed in occupations which require that they "labour with [their] head[s]" may be given "two or more votes" at the polls (1861b 336). He thus advocates public testing to determine the weight each individual's political opinion should carry; he says that, "in this direction lies the true ideal of representative government" (1861b, 337).

Of course, it must be acknowledged that Mill does not endorse policies that *withhold* suffrage from anybody, he is only suggesting that some especially intelligent persons be awarded more than a single vote. Yet, the practice of giving certain individuals voting power greater than that of a single vote is, in effect, equivalent to withholding suffrage from those awarded the power of only a single vote, and is thus a significant departure from democracy. So again, we find that utilitarian liberalism harbors illiberal potentialities.

This admittedly quick tour through three dominant versions of comprehensive liberalism can be seen as a dialectical progression away from robust philosophical foundations. Beginning with the theological doctrine employed by Locke, which promoted a divine justification for liberalism, liberal theory has been forced by its own commitments to retreat to a more modest theoretical ground. However, this dialectic is not solely historical, even if it manifested itself historically. It exists within the aspirations of comprehensive liberalism itself. On the one hand, a liberal theory should be thick enough to provide a strong justification for liberalism. On the other hand, a liberal theory should be thin enough to not produce conflicts with the liberal political commitments. The former requirement drives the liberal theorist to adopt robust philosophical foundations; the latter pushes in the opposite direction, forcing the liberal theorist to try to get along with as little philosophy as possible.

The ideal liberal theory, then, will have to somehow coordinate these seemingly incompatible aims. That is, an ideal comprehensive theory will attempt to locate and employ philosophical foundations which are at once thick enough to provide a justification for liberalism stronger and more secure than that supplied by the utilitarian view, and general enough to win the assent of free persons who harbor a plurality of diverse philosophical, moral, and theological doctrines. The stage has been set for an examination of contemporary liberal philosophy, and especially the early work of John Rawls, whose theory of "justice as fairness" attempts to derive a roughly Kantian liberalism directly from the choice-theoretic concept of a rational agent.

Rawls's Comprehensive Liberalism

Rawls is often credited with singlehandedly restoring and reinvigorating the enterprise of political philosophy. It is often said that *A Theory of Justice* (TJ) marks a return to grand-scale philosophical analysis of substantive questions of political theory. Within its pages are developed systematic accounts of distributive justice, the grounds of political legitimacy, and the relation of political rights to individual goods that are not only philosophically rigorous, but also attentive to important developments in related disciplines such as economics and decision theory. Jonathan Wolff's claim, "before Rawls there were only two options in political philosophy: utilitarianism, or no theory at all" (1998, 120), captures nicely what seems to be the general opinion among contemporary political philosophers.[12]

Describing his own project in TJ, Rawls states, "During much of modern moral philosophy, the predominant systematic theory has been some form of utilitarianism." He contends that, although the utilitarians have been duly criticized for various ambiguities in their doctrine, a "workable and systematic" alternative theory has not yet been produced (TJ, xvii). Rawls's objective is to "offer an alternative systematic account of justice that is superior . . . to the dominant utilitarianism of the tradition" (TJ, xviii).[13] The resulting theory is "highly Kantian in nature" (TJ, xviii), although neither rooted in, nor dependent upon, the discredited metaphysics of transcendental idealism. Rawls aims to "detach" Kantian liberalism from its "metaphysical surroundings" (TJ, 233) and propose a nonutilitarian theory of justice grounded within a "reasonable empiricist framework" (1996, 285) that is "relatively free from objection" (TJ, 233; cf. 226).

Hence, one may read TJ as an attempt to satisfy two desiderata. First, Rawls wants to establish liberalism on ground firmer than that supplied by utilitarianism; that is, he wants a theory of justice which can acknowledge that "Each person possesses an inviolability founded on justice that even the welfare of society as a whole cannot override" (TJ, 3), and so can maintain that principles of justice "are not contingent upon existing desires or present social conditions" (TJ, 232). Second, Rawls wants to eschew Kantian metaphysics; the inviolability of persons and the noncontingency of the principles of justice are not to rest upon "*a priori* considerations" (TJ, 231), but rather are to follow from "the most general assumptions" (TJ, 239) that are "weak and widely held" (TJ, 214).

The leading features of Rawls's theory of Justice as Fairness are by now well known, so we shall not review the details of the view, but focus instead on the justificatory strategy it employs.[14] Rawls proposes to restore the contractarian tradition by employing the concept of a social contract at an "order of abstraction" (TJ, xviii) higher than that of his predecessors. The heightened abstraction is supposed to allay the standard objections raised against contractarianism. The idea, common to traditional contract theories, that the origin and justification of government rests in a social contract between autonomous and self-interested persons in a presocial state of nature has been criticized at least since Hume for being a mere fiction.[15] As real political legitimacy cannot emerge from an imagined contract between imaginary persons, critics argue that the device of a social contract is theoretically impotent.

Rawls employs the idea of the social contract in a way that avoids this difficulty. On Rawls's view, the contract is an "expository device" (TJ, 19), not an explanation of the origin or justification of government and law. According to Rawls, we are to analyze questions of justice from the point of view of "free and rational" parties "concerned to further their own interests" (TJ, 10) who enter into an original contract under conditions specially contrived to ensure that the contract is fair. Should one demonstrate that a given principle of justice would be chosen by such parties contracting under the specified conditions of fairness, one will have thereby demonstrated its correctness (TJ, 12).[16]

The claim that the original contract must be established under conditions of fairness constitutes another important deviation from traditional contractarianism. Whereas the earlier theorists postulated a state of nature in which persons, fully aware of their interests and desires, bargained for terms which would best serve their individual advantage, Rawls maintains that questions of justice are to be examined from an "original position" which features a "veil of ignorance" that deprives the contracting parties of information about themselves and their particular desires. In the original position,

> No one knows his place in society, his class position, or social status, nor does any one know his fortune in the distribution of natural assets and abilities, his intelligence, strength, and the like. (TJ, 11)

Rawls additionally stipulates that the veil deprives the parties of information regarding their "conceptions of the good" and their "special psychological propensities" (TJ, 11). In this way, the veil corrects for "the arbitrariness of the world" (TJ, 122) by guaranteeing that "no one is advantaged or disadvantaged in the choice of principles by the outcome of natural chance or the contingency of social circumstances" (TJ, 11). Although the parties in the original position are self-interested, the veil nullifies "the effects of specific contingencies which put men at odds and tempt them to exploit social and natural circumstances to their own advantage" (TJ, 118). Rawls explains further:

Since all are similarly situated and no one is able to design principles to favor his particular condition, the principles of justice are the
result of a fair agreement or bargain. (TJ, 11)

In short, Justice as Fairness maintains that any principles of justice that
would be agreed to by free, rational, and self-interested parties situated behind a veil of ignorance are ipso facto valid principles of justice. Put most
generally, according to Justice as Fairness, any principle agreed to under fair
conditions of deliberation is a just principle. Hence the name.

The bulk of TJ is devoted to demonstrating that, if presented with the
task of determining the fundamental rules of distributive justice for the
basic structure[17] of society, free and rational parties situated behind
the veil of ignorance and concerned to further their own interests would
choose exactly two principles. These two principles are therefore, on
Rawls's view, proper principles of justice for the basic structure of society.
The two principles Rawls believes would be chosen in the original position are given various formulations in TJ. The final formulations in the
book are as follows.

First Principle of Justice
Each person is to have an equal right to the most extensive total system of
equal basic liberties compatible with a similar system of liberty for all.

Second Principle of Justice
Social and economic inequalities are to be arranged so that they are both as
follows:

1. To the greatest benefit of the least advantaged, consistent with the
   just savings principle, and
2. Attached to offices and positions open to all under conditions of fair
   equality of opportunity[18] (TJ, 266).

In the original 1971 edition of TJ, Rawls summarized his two principles,
along with the appropriate priority rules, into a single-sentence "general
conception." Although this concise formulation has been curiously omitted
from the revised 1999 edition, it is especially clear and warrants citation.
Rawls writes:

All social primary goods—liberty, opportunity, income, and wealth,
and the bases of self-respect—are to be distributed equally unless an
unequal distribution of any or all of these goods is to the advantage
of the least favored.[19]

Commentators have yet to reach consensus on the specific economic and political implications of Rawls's theory of justice. Moreover, the precise meaning of these principles of justice continues to be the source of considerable debate among sympathizers and critics. We shall not review these controversies. It is tempting, nevertheless, to raise the following objection: How are we to suppose that parties in the original position would choose principles that Rawls himself cannot adequately formulate? Presumably, parties to the contract would have to formulate principles and reckon their likely implications for the basic economic and political structure of their society before they could possibly deliberate about them, much less agree to them. Principles ambiguous in both formulation and implication could no more be agreed to in the original position than principles announced in a foreign language.

This kind of objection is misguided, but instructively so. The objection misconstrues the intended role of the original position in Rawls's theory. We must remember that the original position is not a device of explanation, but of reflection; that is, Rawls is not committed to some empirical hypothesis when he claims that parties situated in the original position would select his principles of justice. He is therefore not vulnerable to the objection. The original position is an imagined vantage point from which we are to evaluate and refine our ideas about justice in a process of moral reflection aiming at what Rawls calls "reflective equilibrium" (TJ, 18); one should thus expect continued revisions and refinements of formulation.[20]

Recall that Rawls seeks a liberal theory grounded in an empirical theory that provides a necessary ground for the liberal principles. That is, Rawls wants to forge a *via media* between a Kantian liberalism that rests upon a transcendental metaphysics of *a priori* necessary truths, and a utilitarian liberalism that indeed avoids excessive metaphysics, but can provide only a contingent and precarious ground for liberalism. Does Justice as Fairness satisfy these requirements? One way to begin to examine this question is to consider the fundamental premise underlying Rawls's contractarian strategy. Rawls formulates this premise as follows: "The choice which rational men would make in this hypothetical situation of equal liberty [i.e., the original position] . . . determines the principles of justice" (TJ, 11). There is a troubling ambiguity in this claim. Suppose for the sake of argument that Rawls's two principles would in fact be chosen in the original position by rational and self-interested parties. Rawls thinks that this fact entails that the two principles are valid principles of justice. In other words, Rawls contends that, in the original position, moral status is connected to choice worthiness. It is not clear why this should be so. What is the precise nature of this supposed connection?

There are at least two interpretations of the connection, and, in TJ, Rawls is unclear as to which he intends to endorse. Consider the following ways of construing the connection between choice worthiness and justice:

1. The fact that a principle would be chosen in the original position is *constitutive* of its justice.
2. The fact that a principle would be chosen in the original position is *evidence* of its justice.

We may call the former the "constitutive" interpretation since it says that connection between the choice worthiness of a principle in the original position and the moral status of that principle is an essential connection. In the joint act of choosing a principle in the original position, parties *confer* justice upon it; choice worthiness in the original position is *constitutive* of the justice of a principle. On the constitutive interpretation, then, a strict proof that the parties would choose a given principle is equivalent to a proof of its justice.

Call the second option the "evidential" interpretation. On this view, the fact that a principle would be chosen in the original position does not strictly constitute its justice, but rather provides warrant for accepting that principle as a valid normative principle. According to the evidential interpretation, the likelihood that a principle would be chosen in the original position bears an evidential relation to the justice of that principle: being a choice worthy principle in the original position is symptomatic of being a just principle; that parties would choose a given principle is an *indication* of its justice. The greater the likelihood that the principle would be chosen, the greater the evidence for its justice. Were one able to demonstrate that some given principle would be chosen in the original position, one would have strong evidence of the justice of that principle, and therefore, be justified in adopting it.

Hence, Rawls must assert either that there is a strong, constitutive connection between choice in the original position and the justice of the chosen principles, or he must assert the weaker, evidential connection. In TJ, one finds support for both interpretations.

The constitutive interpretation is supported by claims like the one cited previously in which Rawls asserts that the parties' choice "determines" the principle of justice (TJ, 11). Elsewhere, Rawls more explicitly adopts the following constitutive interpretation:

> To say that a certain conception of justice would be chosen in the original position is *equivalent* to saying that rational deliberation

satisfying certain conditions and restrictions would reach a certain conclusion. (TJ, 119–120, my emphasis)

The constitutive interpretation is supported further by Rawls's claim that justice as fairness is based upon "the notion of pure procedural justice" (TJ, 118). In a choice situation involving pure procedural justice,

> There is no independent criterion for the right result; instead, there is a correct or fair procedure such that the outcome is likewise correct or fair, *whatever it is,* provided that the procedure has been followed. (TJ, 75, my emphasis)

Hence, "The original position is defined in such a way that it is a status quo in which any agreements reached are fair" (TJ, 104). Since in Justice as Fairness, a fair agreement is necessarily just, any agreement in the original position will be just (TJ, 118). On the constitutive interpretation, then, "the principles of justice are not thought of as self-evident, but have their justification in the fact that they would be chosen" (TJ, 37).

Alternatively, the evidential interpretation is supported by Rawls's description of the original position as an "intuitive" (TJ, 19) device. Rawls explains,

> One should not be mislead, then, by the somewhat unusual conditions that characterize the original position. The idea here is simply to make vivid to ourselves the restrictions that it seems reasonable to impose on arguments for principles of justice, and therefore, on these principles themselves. (TJ, 16)

The original position thus "collect[s] together into one conception" the "conditions on principles that we are ready upon due consideration to recognize as reasonable" (TJ, 19). Hence, the original position serves as a "natural guide to intuition"; it is a "perspective" that "one can at any time adopt" (TJ, 120) which conforms to our "considered judgments" (TJ, 105) about justice and thus allows us to "envision our objective from afar" (TJ, 19). Hence, "The reasoning [in the original position] is informal and not a proof, and there is an appeal to intuition as the basis of the theory of justice" (TJ, 159, my emphasis).

On the evidential view suggested by these remarks, choice in the original position derives its normative force from the fact that it embodies our intuitive sense of justice. Since certain intuitive normative premises are built into the construct of the original position, the fact that a principle would be chosen there provides evidence of its justice. The original position, on this view, is a heuristic instrument of moral epistemology; it helps us to see or discover the principles of justice.

Interestingly, these two interpretations of the connection between choice in the original position and justice correspond roughly to the two ways Rawls argues more systematically for his principles of justice. On the one hand, Rawls suggests that one may argue that his two principles cohere well with "our considered judgments of justice." On the other hand, Rawls claims that "one can also find arguments in their favor that are decisive from the standpoint of the original position" (TJ, 132) via the maximin strategy. The former kind of argument suggests the evidential interpretation, whereas the latter recommends the constitutive view.

The ambiguity in TJ with regard to these competing interpretations can be seen as the product of the fundamental tension with that I contend is endemic to liberalism. The constitutive view draws upon a tacit but robust philosophical theory of the person whereas the evidential interpretation attempts to circumvent philosophy by appealing strictly to our intuitions. However, as I shall now argue, neither view satisfies Rawls's desiderata—he must either make explicit the justification for his premises, or he must be content with a theory that offers little advantage over a utilitarian liberalism.

On the constitutive interpretation, one will have to explain why it is the case that choice, under the unusual conditions modeled in the original position, is constitutive of justice. That is, the constitutive view prompts the question: What is distinctive about the original position such that any principle chosen there will *ipso facto* be just? Traditional contract theorists had an easy answer to this question. On traditional versions of the contract theory, the state of nature models a conception of human nature.[21] Persons in this state are natural, and motivated by the desire to exercise and preserve their natural freedom. Decisions and deliberations in the state of nature thus express the characteristic features of human nature. As political associations are artificial means to preserving as much natural freedom as is consistent with the security and protection for all, the political arrangements that would be chosen or consented to by humans in their most natural state are just. Traditional contractarianism thus defers to a theory of human nature to provide the essential connection between choice and justice in the state of nature.

This strategy is not immediately open to Rawls, who is wary of "controversial ethical elements" (TJ, 12) and wants a theory which employs only "weak and widely held" (TJ, 214) presumptions that are "natural and plausible" (TJ, 16) because they are embedded within the "framework of an empirical theory" (TJ, 226). However, he needs *some* account of the supposedly essential connection between choice and justice, and he apparently relies upon rational choice theory to establish this (TJ, 14–15). But this appeal to rational choice theory does not answer the question, it merely delays it. *Why* is the framework of rational choice theory appropriate for a theory of justice? Unless one claims that rational choice theory effectively captures something about human nature that is relevant to questions of justice, our initial question—namely, why is choice in the original position constitutive of the justice of the principles chosen—remains unanswered.

One could, of course, argue on Kantian grounds that rational choice theory does capture something about human nature that is particularly relevant to justice. A Kantian may argue that humans are by nature autonomous, and that any political arrangement that can be shown to accord with the autonomous nature of humans is *ipso facto* just. Since the most basic exercise of individual autonomy is rational, uncoerced choice, and since justice simply is that which would be autonomously chosen, any principle chosen in the original position is necessarily just. Although this Kantian response does indeed explain the constitutive connection between rational choice and justice in the original position, it is clear that Rawls cannot employ this kind of argument if he is to avoid controversial premises, for it invokes an entire theory of human nature.

The relevant point is that the constitutive interpretation will necessarily involve some such theory, and will thus drive Rawls to articulate, or quietly endorse, the kind of controversial theory of human nature he wants to avoid. Taking the constitutive view of the original position will therefore frustrate the desire to remain within the confines of empirical theory. Rawls's interest in avoiding metaphysics will therefore draw him toward the evidential interpretation.

On the evidential interpretation, the original position is a heuristic device embodying our intuitive and considered sense of justice. On this view, justice as fairness is indeed a strictly empirical theory since questions of what liberals do in fact tend to think about justice are empirical questions. However, the evidential interpretation renders Rawls's theory of justice surprisingly incomplete.

On the evidential view, the position developed in TJ is not strictly a theory of justice at all; it is rather, as Rawls says, "A theory of our moral sentiments as manifested by our considered judgments" (TJ, 104). That is, Rawls does not provide a demonstration of the two principles, but simply proposes a model of moral reasoning that helps to clarify and organize the commonsense, intuitive sense of justice likely to be held by persons who favor liberalism. Accordingly, Rawls admits, "We want to define the original position so that we get the desired solution" (TJ, 122).[22] The desired solution derives from the liberal conception of justice which the original position models. On the evidential interpretation, Rawls presupposes the validity of a liberal conception of justice. His argument consists not in demonstrating this conception, but in showing that it commits liberals to his two principles of distribution.

On the evidential interpretation, then, a positive case for liberalism is entirely absent from TJ. But this leaves the liberal intuitions about justice unscrutinized and entirely unsupported. The evidential interpretation, therefore, frustrates Rawls's desire to provide a ground for liberalism firmer than that supplied by utilitarianism. His case for his principles of justice rests entirely upon the presumed validity of the liberal intuitions from which he begins. Should it turn out that Rawls has misidentified or misrepresented the intuitive sense of justice shared by liberals, his theory will collapse. Furthermore, his theory of justice can engage only those who are already well disposed to liberalism; his theory is unable to convert antiliberals to liberalism.

To review: TJ invites two incompatible interpretations of the connections between choice and justice in the original position. I named these the *constitutive* and the *evidential* interpretations. I then argued that neither interpretation satisfies Rawls's desire both to avoid metaphysics and to produce a stronger case for liberalism than utilitarianism offers. The constitutive interpretation forces Rawls to adopt and employ the kind of metaphysical and ethical presumptions he wishes to avoid. The evidential interpretation is problematic because it leaves Rawls without any firm ground for his liberalism, and therefore, constitutes no real advantage over a utilitarian theory. Whereas the utilitarian derives the liberal principles from considerations concerning existing social conditions and utility distributions, Rawls rests his case for liberalism entirely upon a precarious appeal to a nebulous set of intuitions. Therefore, neither interpretation is satisfactory from the point of view of Rawls's desiderata.

This difficulty in Rawls's argument has generated great controversy.[23] Troubled by the prospect that the pioneering work of political philosophy in the twentieth century could be a grand *petitio principii*, sympathetic and critical commentators have endeavored to uncover the "hidden assumptions" (Dworkin 1973, 26) underlying Rawls's view and to unlock the "secret of the original position" (Sandel 1982, 132).

Typically, those sympathetic to liberalism have argued that the evidential interpretation of the original position is correct, and consequently that Rawls's view presupposes, rather than proves, the validity of liberalism and its characteristic moral claims. On this, Thomas Nagel is clear:

> The egalitarian liberalism which [Rawls] develops and the conception of the good on which it depends are extremely persuasive, but the original position serves to model rather than to justify them . . .

> I believe that Rawls' conclusions can be more persuasively defended
> by direct moral arguments for liberty and equality . . . . (1973, 15)

Ronald Dworkin argues similarly,

> The two principles comprise a theory of justice that is built up from
> the hypothesis of a contract. But the contract cannot sensibly be
> taken as the fundamental premise or postulate of that theory . . . It
> must be seen as a kind of halfway point in a larger argument, as it-
> self the product of a deeper political theory . . . We must therefore
> try to identify the features of a deeper theory that would recom-
> mend the device of a contract as the engine of justice . . . . (1973,
> 37)[24]

These commentators have faced an obvious difficulty. If it is true that
Rawls's "conclusions can be more persuasively defended by direct moral arguments" and that we must search for the "deeper theory" his presentation
presupposes, then why should Rawls have elected to adopt a contractarian
strategy in the first place? Why did he bother with the idea of the original
position at all? This kind of defense of Rawls renders the construct of the
original position, the element that seemed to lie at the heart of Rawls's argument, a curious and superfluous adjunct to Justice as Fairness.

Many of Rawls's critics have adopted the constitutive interpretation.
They have argued that Rawls's view presupposes an entire metaphysics of
the self, which, once uncovered, is vulnerable to decisive objections. The
strongest articulation of this kind of critique is found in the work of
Michael Sandel.[25] In *Liberalism and the Limits of Justice*, Sandel argues that
Rawls's depiction of the parties in the original position commits him to a
roughly Kantian theory of the self. On this view, the self is a detached "subject of possession" (1982, 59) for which no commitment or obligation arising from a social relation could constitute identity. According to Sandel,
since Rawls maintains that "the self is prior to the ends which are affirmed
by it" (TJ, 491), he must also assert the following:

> No commitment could grip me so deeply that I could not under-
> stand myself without it. No transformation of life purposes and
> plans could be so unsettling as to disrupt the contours of my iden-
> tity. No project could be so essential that turning away from it would
> call into question the person I am. (Sandel 1982, 62)

That is, Sandel argues that Rawls is committed to a theory according to
which the self is essentially "unencumbered" by social relations, given
"prior to and independent of its purposes and ends . . . unbound by prior
moral ties, capable of choosing [its] ends for [itself]" (1996, 12).

On Sandel's view, then, Rawls has failed to articulate a theory confined to an empirical framework. Moreover, Sandel argues that the metaphysical picture of the self, presupposed by Rawls, is demonstrably false. According to Sandel, the image of the unencumbered self "fails to capture those loyalties and responsibilities whose moral force consists partly in the fact that living by them is inseparable from understanding ourselves as the particular persons we are" (1996, 14; cf. 1982, 179). Certain obligations, Sandel contends, are such that they cannot be properly understood as the product of the choice of an unencumbered self. The force of religious, familial, and patriotic duties and loyalties, lies precisely in the fact that these are given and not chosen. The theory of the unencumbered self cannot account for these most important and "indispensable aspects of our moral and political experience" (1996, 14).

Finally, Sandel argues that Rawls must tacitly reject the theory of the unencumbered self if his second principle of justice is to make sense. Recall that the second of Rawls's principles stipulates that economic goods are to be redistributed so that inequalities are to the advantage of the least well off. According to Rawls, this scheme of distribution "represents, in effect, an agreement to regard the distribution of natural talents as in some respects a common asset" (TJ, 87). Sandel argues that there is no basis for regarding the natural distribution of individual talents a "common asset" unless we "presuppose some prior moral tie" among the individuals whose talents would be enlisted in a "communal endeavor" (1984b, 22) of the sort envisioned by the theory of the self which Rawls rejects. Sandel concludes that Rawls's theory is "parasitic" on a theory of the encumbered self and the corresponding constitutive theory of community it "officially rejects" (1984b, 24; cf. 1982, 80). In short, Sandel argues that Rawls presupposes a theory of the self that is not only false, but insufficient for his own liberal purposes.

The tension within TJ is yet another instantiation of the tension within liberal theory generally. The two interpretations of the original position map neatly on two opposing liberal justificatory strategies. One, embodied in the evidential interpretation, presumes a set of intuitive basic liberal principles and proceeds to build a theory of liberal justice upon considered judgments. Accordingly, the justification of liberalism offered by this strategy is philosophically modest, but for that reason perhaps able to appeal to a wide variety of persons; it is in this sense attentive to the pressures of social pluralism on liberal theorizing. The second, embodied in the constitutive interpretation, relies upon an argument grounded in specific conceptions of rationality and the self. This view consequently harbors deep philosophical commitments and its justificatory aspirations are more robust. But, it is not free from the kind of metaphysical commitments Rawls wants to avoid, and, as Sandel argues, not able to recognize the full range of ways in which selves are related to each other and their own moral commitments; it is, in this sense, insufficiently pluralistic.

In TJ, Rawls runs both kinds of justification in tandem, sometimes relying heavily upon rational choice theory and elsewhere appealing strictly to considered judgments in reflective equilibrium. But these two kinds of justification do not really complement each other. If the proper interpretation of the original position is constitutive, our considered judgments have very little to do with political theorizing about justice. If, alternatively, the proper understanding of the original position is evidential, then our intuitions are decisive, and there is no point in appealing to the rational choice apparatus. The tension in liberal theory remains unresolved.

CHAPTER 4
Three Liberal Responses

The argument of the previous two chapters has demonstrated an internal tension within comprehensive liberal theory. I have framed this tension in terms of a conflict between the social pluralism that is the outcome of liberal *political practice* and liberal theory's deeply philosophical conception of legitimacy. Stated baldly, liberalism holds that public consensus, upon the fundamental normative principles of a political order, is required for the legitimacy of that order; however, liberalism is also committed to the view that within a free society, one should expect to find a plurality of conflicting normative visions. Where such pluralism exists, there could be little groundwork upon which to base wide consensus on any particular normative principles. Liberalism's pluralism frustrates its own theory of legitimacy.

We shall now consider three recent liberal attempts to navigate the tension. One strategy, taken by John Rawls in his later work, is to develop a new style of liberal theory, one that gives up the philosophical and universalist aspirations of liberal theory. Another strategy, taken by William Galston, is to use pluralism itself as the philosophical foundation of a comprehensive liberal theory. A third strategy, taken by Richard Rorty, is to abandon the project of liberal theory altogether. The argument of this chapter will be that none of these liberal responses is satisfactory. We shall proceed by taking each in turn.

Political Liberalism
John Rawls's later work is driven by the tension that I have identified within liberal theory. Again, the details of his political liberalism are well-known

and will not be rehearsed here.[1] It is important, however, to underscore the contrast in the justificatory structure between political liberalism and traditional comprehensive approaches. As we have seen, comprehensive liberalisms adopt what I have called the *philosophical* aspiration of liberal theory; that is, that attempt to establish the legitimacy of a liberal political order by means of a demonstration of the principal liberal commitments from philosophical premises. Comprehensive liberalisms, therefore, expect wide consensus upon those philosophical premises.

By contrast, political liberalism begins from the identification of the "fact of reasonable pluralism" (1996, 4).[2] Rawls characterizes the fact of reasonable pluralism as follows:

> Under political and social conditions secured by the basic rights and liberties of free institutions, a diversity of conflicting and irreconcilable—and what's more, reasonable—comprehensive doctrines will come about and persist if such diversity does not already obtain. (1996, 36)

The fact of reasonable pluralism implies a second fact, the "fact of oppression":

> [A] continuing shared understanding on one comprehensive religious, moral, or philosophical doctrine can be maintained only by the oppressive use of state power. (1996, 37)

In short, Rawls contends that "the fact of free institutions is the fact of pluralism" (1989, 474); and "free institutions themselves lead to pluralism" (1989, 491).

When coupled with the "liberal principle of legitimacy" (1996, 136), the fact of reasonable pluralism entails the rejection of comprehensive theories of liberalism, and the need for a noncomprehensive liberal theory. To explain: Liberals maintain that since political power is always coercive power (1996, 216), consent is essential to the legitimacy of a political order:

> [. . .]our exercise of political power is proper and hence justifiable only when it is exercised in accordance with a constitution the essentials of which all citizens may reasonably be expected to endorse in the light of principles and ideals acceptable to them as reasonable and rational. (1996, 217)

However, the fact of reasonable pluralism means that there is no comprehensive theory upon which all rational and reasonable persons will converge; hence, the justification of liberal political power and institutions cannot lie within some philosophical view. Any society whose institutions presuppose any particular philosophical doctrine—even a decidedly *liberal* one—will *ipso facto* be illiberal.

Therefore, the very idea of a comprehensive liberalism is incoherent: The fact of pluralism entails that comprehensive theories are self-refuting. "The question the dominant tradition has tried to answer has no answer: No comprehensive doctrine is appropriate as a political conception for a constitutional regime" (1996, 135). According to Rawls, the main question of liberal philosophy is not what philosophical account best establishes the legitimacy of a liberal order, but rather, how it is possible for there to exist over time "a just and stable society of free and equal citizens who remain profoundly divided by reasonable religious, philosophical, and moral doctrines" (1996, 4).

Given the fact of reasonable pluralism and the "absolute depth" of the "irreconcilable latent conflict" among reasonable citizens in any free society (1996, xxvi), only an account of the basic structure of a liberal-democratic society, which is political in that it is "independent of controversial philosophical and religious doctrines" (1985, 388) could be legitimate. However, Rawls is quick to insist that a political account of liberalism must not be "political in the wrong way" (1996, 142). That is, Rawls contends that if a liberal society is to be stable, citizens must be committed to the basic principles of liberalism on grounds that run deeper than those Rawls characterizes as a *modus vivendi* agreement (1996, 145). Where liberalism is accepted among citizens as a *modus vivendi,* each sees liberalism as a second best compromise. For such citizens, the best state of affairs would be a political arrangement that reflected completely their own comprehensive doctrine. Accordingly, a liberal society based upon a *modus vivendi* will be unstable because the "form and content" of its basic principles will be contingent upon "the existing balance of political power" among the competing comprehensive doctrines (1996, 142).

Therefore, the stability of a liberal society cannot lie within general agreement upon a single comprehensive doctrine and it cannot lie within a *modus vivendi* agreement among citizens. From whence shall it derive? Rawls proposes that if liberal society is to be stable, it must formulate its basic commitments in terms that can be the focus of an "overlapping consensus" among the comprehensive doctrines endorsed by its reasonable citizens. Where the basics of a liberal regime are the focus of an overlapping consensus, each reasonable citizen sees the basic principles of his society as an appropriate manifestation in the political realm of his own comprehensive doctrine. In this way, Rawls aims to formulate a conception of liberalism that can serve as a "module, an essential constituent part" that "fits into and can be supported by various reasonable comprehensive doctrines that endure in the society governed by it" (1996, 12). Hence, citizens will endorse the liberal arrangement "for its own sake" and "on its own merits," not as a second-best compromise (1996, 148).

The main argument running through Rawls's later work can now be stated succinctly. Rawls endeavors to show that his preferred version of liberalism, Justice as Fairness, when properly formulated in the light of the fact of reasonable pluralism, is the only conception of the basic principles of a liberal regime that can win an overlapping consensus among contemporary citizens in democratic societies. However, there is reason to think that Rawls's proposal is, in fact, incoherent.

The concept of reasonableness plays a multifaceted role in Rawls's proposal. In the first place, free institutions do not merely generate *pluralism* at the level of comprehensive doctrines, but a pluralism of reasonable comprehensive views.[3] Additionally, reasonable citizens are those who affirm reasonable comprehensive doctrines (1996, 36). Rawls also employs the concept of reasonableness in identifying the set of persons whose consent is necessary for the legitimacy of a liberal regime. Rawls maintains that a liberal regime is legitimate only if it can win the consent of the reasonable citizens to whom it is proposed, the consent of unreasonable citizens is not necessary for legitimacy.

As it lies at the very heart of Rawls's political liberalism, we must examine the idea of reasonableness. According to Rawls, a citizen is reasonable only if he (1) accepts the fact of reasonable pluralism and (2) "is willing to propose and honor fair terms of cooperation" to govern his dealings with those with whom he profoundly disagrees at the level of comprehensive views (1996, 49 n. 1). Accordingly, it is unreasonable to insist that the terms of social cooperation conform to one's own comprehensive view. Likewise, it is unreasonable to demand that state power be used to enforce the principles of one's own comprehensive doctrine (1996, 65): "Where there is a plurality of reasonable doctrines, it is unreasonable or worse to want to use the sanctions of state power to correct, or to punish, those who disagree with us" (1996, 138).

The reasonable person therefore acknowledges the fact of reasonable pluralism; that is, he recognizes that at least some of those persons holding comprehensive views that are incompatible with his own have reasons for believing as they do which are as good as his reasons for holding his own view. Moreover, the reasonable person seeks to establish and maintain fair terms of social cooperation with such persons. Insofar as these other persons are themselves reasonable, they too accept the fact of reasonable pluralism and seek fair terms of cooperation. They all recognize that to accomplish this, one must refrain from proposing terms of political association that are couched in one's own comprehensive doctrine. Instead, one should instead attempt to cast all proposals for political arrangement in a vocabulary that is neutral and mutually agreeable to all. As they are divided on philosophical, moral, and religious essentials, only those political principles and arrangements that do not presuppose or draw upon any particular philosophical, moral, or religious conceptions will be mutually agreeable. They thus devise and accept a collection of arrangements and principles that do not draw upon any particular comprehensive doctrine. But this is to say that reasonable persons are necessarily political liberals. Stronger still, it is to say that *only* political liberals are reasonable persons, and that the consent of political liberals is sufficient for political legitimacy.

Rawls will respond that the comprehensive doctrines associated with, for example, Kant and Mill have "their proper place in the background culture" of a free society and can play a "supporting role" in a regime of political liberalism (1996, 211 n. 42). He will thus deny that according to political liberalism, the Millian and the Kantian are unreasonable. He will likewise deny that political liberalism excludes Kantians and Millians from the "legitimation pool," namely, the "pool of persons whose endorsement would confirm the legitimacy of Rawls's political liberalism" (M. Friedman 2000, 16).

Yet, it is unclear that Rawls can maintain this with consistency. Consider the simple utilitarian. According to him, state action and policy are *just* only insofar as they maximize general happiness. Furthermore, he maintains that a state is legitimate only if it abides by the dictates of justice. Therefore, insofar as he believes that the state must be legitimate, the utilitarian contends that the state must endeavor to maximize general happiness. Should the state decide policy on grounds other than the Greatest Happiness Principle, it will be, according to the utilitarian, unjust and illegitimate. Yet according Rawls, it is unreasonable to expect the state to endorse one's own comprehensive doctrine. Therefore, because he expects state action to satisfy the Greatest Happiness Principle, the utilitarian is unreasonable according to the political liberal.

Rawls will respond that whereas in a liberal society citizens are free to endorse and follow any reasonable comprehensive view in their private lives, they are unreasonable if they expect state policy to always reflect their own doctrine. This means that whereas the utilitarian is fully reasonable in his belief that right actions are those that maximize the general good, he is unreasonable if he believes that this conception should be adopted in the political realm. That is, in order to be reasonable, one must recognize the political as a "special domain" (1989, 482) separate from nonpolitical realms and having its own distinct values that "normally will have sufficient weight to override all other values that may come into conflict with them" (1989, 483).

So, the utilitarian may believe that persons should seek to maximize general happiness; however, he must not insist that the state adopt this view.

Moreover, whereas the utilitarian may believe that his conceptions of morality and justice are *true*, he must not insist that they be given any political force. But is this possible? Rawls writes,

> It is vital to the idea of political liberalism that we may with perfect consistency hold that it would be unreasonable to use political power to enforce our own comprehensive view, which we must, of course, affirm as either reasonable or true. (1996, 138)

On Rawls's view, then, to qualify as reasonable, the utilitarian must accept the proposed distinction between the political and nonpolitical domains and must additionally subordinate the specific values associated with utilitarianism to the political values associated with the political domain. So whereas the utilitarian maintains that,

1. Actions and policies are just only if they maximize general happiness.

And he is reasonable *if and only if* he also accepts that,

2. It is not the case that in deciding action and policy, the state must try to maximize general happiness.

Thus, on Rawls's view, the reasonable utilitarian believes,

3. A state may be legitimate even though it does not always strive to do what is just.

This seems incoherent. Part of what makes utilitarianism a comprehensive philosophical view is that it proposes its own conception of political justice and its own distinction between the political and the nonpolitical. So whereas it is possible for someone to believe both (1) and (2), it is not possible for a *utilitarian* to do so. If he accepts (2), he ceases to be a utilitarian. As Rawls maintains that rejecting (2) would render the utilitarian unreasonable, it follows that, according to Rawls, utilitarians are unreasonable.

Rawls is demanding that the utilitarian revise his position in light of the fact of reasonable pluralism. To be sure, such revision will not require great deviation from the classical utilitarian view; the revision amounts to tempering the proposed scope of the Greatest Happiness Principle so that it applies only to nonpolitical domains. We might even imagine a reformed utilitarian agreeing with Rawls and making the necessary adjustments. But a reformed utilitarian is a compromised utilitarian, and it is unclear why any utilitarian ought to reform his view to accommodate Rawls. More importantly, it is not clear that Rawls can give any nonquestion-begging reason why utilitarians should become reformed utilitarians. Unless he is to defend reasonable pluralism as an independent thesis, thereby plunging into the depths of philosophical controversy, Rawls can offer no principled incentive to the utilitarian to become a reformed utilitarian.

Of course, one reason why utilitarians might reform their view to accommodate the fact of reasonable pluralism is that not doing so will exclude them from the legitimation pool. Recall that according to Rawls, legitimacy is generated by the consent of rational and reasonable persons; the consent of irrational and unreasonable persons is not required for legitimacy. This is to say that the consent of an unreformed utilitarian is not necessary for political legitimacy, and thus that, on Rawls's view, the coercive power of the state may be employed against unreformed utilitarians on the grounds that their comprehensive doctrine is unreasonable.[4] Where a philosophical argument is lacking or otherwise to be avoided, Rawls offers an *ad baculum*.

Thus, it is not the case that those holding unreasonable comprehensive views will merely be excluded from the pool of those whose consent is constitutive of legitimacy. As if exclusion were not enough, Rawls also claims that the politically liberal state may take positive steps to curb the influence of unreasonable comprehensive views. Rawls writes,

> [A] given society may also contain unreasonable, irrational, and even mad, comprehensive doctrines. In their case, the problem is to contain them so that they do not undermine the unity and justice of society. (1996, xvi–xvii)

How does one contain a comprehensive doctrine? Marilyn Friedman answers,

> Doing so requires regulating and controlling the media in which it is expressed and promulgated—books, magazines, cyberspace, and so on. More significantly, it requires suppressing those who hold the doctrine, in particular, suppressing their expression and/or their enactment of it.[5] (2000, 22–23)

Wanting to avoid the consequences of unreasonableness, the utilitarian may elect to become a reformed utilitarian as a matter of political prudence. We may, therefore, speak of the "reluctantly reformed utilitarian" as one who tempers his utilitarianism not because he sees that there is a fact of reasonable pluralism, but simply as a necessary political compromise.

The argument has shown that political liberalism requires utilitarians to reform their view to accommodate the fact of reasonable pluralism and the corresponding political/nonpolitical distinction endorsed by Rawls. Of course, the political liberal cannot offer the utilitarian any philosophical arguments to support the proposed revision of utilitarianism; doing so would induce the kind of philosophical controversy the political liberal wishes to avoid. We have seen, however, that political liberalism does offer the utilitarian an incentive for reforming his view—the political liberal may employ the state's coercive power to quell unreasonable comprehensive doctrines. As a matter of prudence, then, the utilitarian might accept the compromises imposed upon his view by political liberalism—he may become what I have called a reluctantly reformed utilitarian.

This complicated argument clearly can be generalized to show that, on Rawls's view, anyone holding a comprehensive doctrine which specifies a particular conception of political justice and which contains a view regarding how the political should be distinguished from the nonpolitical is unreasonable. To avoid the measures designed to contain their allegedly unreasonable doctrines, those holding such views will reform their respective doctrines to accommodate the fact of reasonable pluralism and the other elements of political liberalism. In doing this, however, they will in part abandon their doctrines. In many cases this reform will be reluctant; that is, persons will accept the required revision of their view as a matter of political compromise.

Yet it is clear that where citizens reluctantly reform their comprehensive views to meet the demands of political liberalism, political liberalism fails to win an overlapping consensus. Citizens will not willingly accept the constraints political liberalism places upon their comprehensive views, but will do so only to avoid the fate of the unreasonable under a politically liberal regime. This is to say that a politically liberal regime can be endorsed only as a *modus vivendi*. As we have seen, Rawls maintains that a *modus vivendi* liberalism is unstable.

Of course, one way to avoid the reluctant reformation of citizens' comprehensive views is to offer a convincing philosophical argument for the fact of reasonable pluralism. If citizens could be convinced that the full exercise of human reason does not ultimately converge upon one comprehensive doctrine, each might be persuaded to accept the terms of a political liberalism. However, this option is certainly not open to Rawls since it would invoke the kind of philosophical controversy he seeks to avoid. If Rawls were to engage in the required philosophical theorizing to establish the fact of reasonable pluralism, he would no longer be a political liberal, but a comprehensive liberal.

Thus, the desiderata expressed by Rawls's political liberalism are not mutually satisfiable. If Rawls wants to fully acknowledge the fact of reasonable pluralism, he must settle for a *modus vivendi* liberalism. If, on the other hand, Rawls wants a stable liberal society (namely, one based upon an overlapping consensus among citizens), he must commit to some deep philosophical claims and thus abandon the idea of a political liberalism. In short, political liberalism is incoherent, and thus an inadequate response to the tension within liberalism.

Pluralist Liberalism

One might think that the mistake made by political liberalism is to infer from the fact of pluralism that one must give up on the idea of a comprehensive liberal theory. The thought here would be that one could formulate a comprehensive theory of liberalism using pluralism itself as the philosophical foundation. This would require that one appeal to pluralism as a *philosophical theory* rather than simply a sociological description. To be a pluralist in this philosophical sense is to propose a particular thesis about certain substantive moral disagreements; specifically, it is to maintain that certain disagreements are permanent and intractable even among fully reasonable and rational persons who sincerely attend to all possible data and every consideration. Following the recent literature, we shall call this philosophical approach to pluralism, *value pluralism.*

According to the value pluralist, the moral facts are themselves in conflict; consequently, there are a number of true moral propositions that do not form a consistent set. This fact about values accounts for the inability of human reason to reach moral consensus. To expect moral consensus among persons is unreasonable.

Value pluralism has important ramifications. First among these is that the very idea of a life manifesting every good available to humans is incoherent. This is not to say that different goods compete for our limited attention and resources, such as when I must decide to contribute a given sum of money either to the arts or to the homeless.[6] It is to say that, even given infinite material, temporal, and epistemic resources, the manifestation of certain actual goods precludes the manifestation, and even the pursuit, of others.[7] Further, if the moral universe consists of a number of distinct and competing goods, then there is no *summum bonum*, no single or highest good, and no common measure by which goods can be ranked or prioritized. Hence, there are varieties of human flourishing and a plurality of human goods, and no way to commensurate them or to resolve conflicts between them.[8]

Given this sketch, the idea of a value pluralist comprehensive liberalism seems problematic: How could the thesis that the moral universe is populated by conflicting and incommensurable values that cannot be rank ordered or subsumed under a single *summum bonum,* entail any definite claims about politics? How could the thesis that the expectation of consensus at the level of deep moral commitment is unreasonable itself form the basis for a liberal theory of politics?

William Galston has recently put forward a comprehensive liberalism rooted in value pluralism. Galston's own views derive from Isaiah Berlin, so we begin with a brief examination of Berlin's argument. Berlin begins from the quasi-existentialist entailment of value pluralism that "the necessity of choosing between absolute claims is . . . an inescapable characteristic of the human condition" (1969, 169). That is, the truth of value pluralism entails that human life inevitably involves choice making among incompatible, competing goods. From this we are to infer that " . . . to be free to choose, and not to be chosen for, is an inalienable ingredient in what makes human beings human" (1969, lx). Because humans realize that they must choose, they consequently value the freedom to choose.[9] In turn, they value a political order that protects this freedom. Therefore, the argument concludes, the liberal state, fixed as it is upon upholding negative liberty, is the most legitimate kind of state. Value pluralism thus entails liberalism.

There are at least two problems here. First, it is unclear how the fact of inevitable choosing among competing goods should lead individuals to value the ability to make such choices freely. In fact, if value pluralism is true, then it is not clear why anyone should value the freedom to choose among goods. Such freedom is valuable only in cases where one must choose between good and bad, or good and less good. But Berlin thinks that the choice between rival goods, not between good and bad, is what is essential, and the incommensurability component of value pluralism disallows rank orderings such as "more good" and "less good" in such cases. Hence, the inference from the inevitability of choice among goods to the valuing of the freedom to make such choices, fails.

Berlin may be simply proposing the anthropological thesis that, as a matter of fact, the acknowledgement of the inevitability of making choices leads individuals to value the freedom to choose. But even if we accept this reading, the argument suffers a second, though related, problem. How does it follow from the fact that individuals value the freedom to choose for themselves among competing goods that the state ought to provide or protect such freedom? The nonpluralist liberal has a clear answer. The state must win the consent of its citizens, and thus must seek to accommodate such demands. Recall that Berlin is supposed to be offering an argument *for* liberalism *from* value pluralism; this line of response is, therefore, not open to him. However, Berlin has no resources for drawing the desired implication; any attempt to explain why the state must respect the desire for freedom of choice will invoke some value that the state must recognize, and any account of why the state must recognize this value will violate value pluralism. Berlin's argument, hence, fails to establish liberalism from pluralist premises.

In recent work, Galston employs a slightly different argument to establish the entailment from value pluralism to liberalism. Summarizing his argument, Galston writes,

> Value pluralism suggests that there is a range of indeterminacy within which various choices are rationally defensible, at least in the sense that they all fall above the ... line of minimum decency. Because there is no single uniquely rational ordering or combination of such values, no one can provide a generally valid reason, binding on all individuals, for a particular ranking or combination. There is, therefore, no rational basis for restrictive policies whose justification includes the assertion that there is a unique rational ordering of value. (2002, 57–58)

Galston cites approvingly Stephen Lukes' (1991, 20) claim that if value pluralism is true, then it would be "unreasonable" for the state to "impose a single [way of life] on some of its citizens" (Galston 2002, 58). Thus, value pluralism entails that any state that goes beyond the protection of negative liberty is unreasonable; hence, value pluralism entails liberalism.

It is not clear that Galston's argument fares better than Berlin's. First note that Galston's argument involves a curious kind of burden shifting. Whereas Berlin contended that value pluralism provides a positive case for liberalism, Galston's argument purports to show that liberalism follows from value pluralism simply because no illiberal order is consistent with the value pluralist thesis. Surely a demonstration that value pluralism entails the rejection of illiberal arrangements is not sufficient for a demonstration of liberalism from value pluralism. Charity prevents an interpretation under which Galston is guilty of this error; the argument must be read as a deliberate attempt to shift the burden of proof to those who would deviate from the liberal norm. The point is that value pluralism defeats the case for illiberal arrangements—there could be no good reason for a state to impose a single way of life upon its citizens. "The value pluralist argument for negative liberty rests on the insufficiency of the reasons typically invoked in favor of restricting it" (2002, 58).

Burden-shifting maneuvers are typically controversial, and this instance is no exception. What entitles Galston to the presumption that liberal negative liberty is properly a default position deviation from which stands in need of justification? Moreover, if negative liberty is taken as a proper default, in what sense is Galston's liberal pluralism a *comprehensive* theory? That is, how does Galtson's liberal pluralism differ from the justificatory structure of Rawlsian political liberalism?

Although I think these are difficult questions for Galston, we need not engage his argument at this level since it is unclear that value pluralism does in fact render illiberal arrangements unreasonable. To see this, imagine three internally consistent, but mutually exclusive and incompossible,[10] clusters of values, A, B, and C. Let us stipulate that clusters A, B, and C each represent a *comprehensive* set of values, what we might call roughly a "way of life," and that each way of life falls above the "line of minimum decency." Let us say that A represents a Millian life of political participation and open-mindedness in the face of a wide variety of experiments in living; B represents a life of devotion, orthodoxy, and service in the name of a traditional religion; and C represents an Emersonian life of self-sufficiency and hard work. Galston's argument has it that there could be no valid reason for a state to promote any of these ways of life among its citizens. The point is intuitive: since A, B, and C are *all* good, there could be no compelling reason to impose, say, A over B, or C rather than A. Thus, the argument runs, the state must allow for A, B, and C, and leave it to citizens to decide which to pursue. In other words, the state has no good reason to do more than protect negative liberty.

But this argument is a muddle. The state indeed has good reason to promote, for example, A, namely that *A is good*. Of course, Galston will insist that the state has no *better* reason for promoting Millian civic liberty rather than religious devotion or Emersonian self-sufficiency, but surely this is *not* a reason for remaining neutral with regard to these options, and it is not a reason to not promote Millian civic liberty. After all, *ex hypothesi*, the Millian way of life is actually good. What could be a better reason for imposing it?

Galston has supposed that the imposition of a Millian way of life will necessarily be accompanied by the claim that it *is exclusively* good, or that its competitors are less good. But it is not clear that this is so, or even that it should matter. There is nothing inconsistent in the idea of a state imposing a single way of life upon its citizens without thereby making any claim about the worth of other ways of life; nor is there anything contradictory about the idea of a state promoting a single way of life while openly acknowledging that other ways of life are also good. But even granting the premise that the imposition of a single way of life must be accompanied by the false claim that it is exclusively good, the implication that imposing a single way of life is unreasonable does not follow.[11]

Galston claims his argument "draws its force from the underlying assumption that coercion always stands exposed to a potential demand for justification" (2002, 58). Explaining further, he writes, "[C]oercion is not a fact of nature, nor is it self-justifying. Just the reverse: There is a presumption against it, grounded in the pervasive human desire to go our own way in accordance with our own desires and beliefs" (2002, 58). In drawing upon a supposedly pervasive human desire to decide for ourselves among competing goods, Galston has now moved closer to the original Berlinian argument, and has inherited its problems.

One may concede that coercion always stands exposed to a potential demand for justification. On the argument I have posed, a state's imposition of a way of life based in Millian civic liberty can be justified by appealing to the fact that the Millian way of life is good. This will be seen as insufficient by Galston, who, like Berlin, locates the force of the demand for justification within the "pervasive human desire to go our own way in accordance with our own desires and beliefs." But why should a value pluralist give any weight to this supposed desire? First, it is not clear that such a desire is reasonable if value pluralism is true. When one is presented with a choice between several irreducibly good, incommensurable, and incompossible options, what sense does it make to desire one rather than another? That is, the desire to go our own way is rational only when the options can be rank ordered. Second, what reason can the value pluralist give for the state to accommodate such desires, especially when doing so opens individuals up to the possibility of living bad lives?

The nonpluralist liberal can give a strong account of why the desire to live in accordance with our own desires and beliefs ought to be accommodated. Such a story will draw upon the overriding value of autonomy, derived generally from the need to feel that one's life is valuable *from the inside* (Kymlicka 1989, 12).[12] The nonpluralist can approve autonomous choice as a kind of trumping value; in this manner, a given individual perceives a way of life, based in Millian civic liberty, as choice-worthy contribution to the value of that way of life for that individual. But this line of argument is not open to the value pluralist, for it involves the claim that autonomy is a trumping value, and that goods can be rank ordered.[13]

Galston's justification for giving weight to the pervasive human desire to go our own way cannot rest upon a standard appeal to autonomy. The most he offers by way of justification is that there is, in fact, a presumption against coercion. Indeed, there is such a presumption *in a liberal political order*. There is certainly no such presumption among those who are not already committed to liberalism. So, as with Berlin, the proposed value pluralist case for liberalism in fact presumes characteristic principles of liberalism that cannot be derived from value pluralism. In this respect, Galston's liberal pluralism is actually a species of political liberalism. Accordingly, Galston has failed to provide a comprehensive liberal theory. More importantly, in adopting the justificatory strategy of Rawlsian political liberalism, Galston's liberal pluralism confronts the same difficulties on which Rawls's ideas were based.

Antifoundationalist Liberalism

I previously argued that political liberalism requires a deep philosophical demonstration of reasonable pluralism and the corresponding distinction between the political and nonpolitical realms if it is to avoid being political in the wrong way. The argument also has shown that if Rawls were to supply the requisite philosophical accounts, his liberal theory would cease to be a political liberalism, and would be a comprehensive liberalism. Someone sympathetic to Rawls's general approach may accept this conclusion. One who approves of Rawls's aspiration to "leave aside philosophical controversies" and to "avoid philosophy's longstanding problems" (1985, 395) could argue that in drawing the distinction between a *modus vivendi* and an overlapping consensus, Rawls made the mistake of indulging in philosophical theorizing. Instead of insisting that liberalism be the focus of an overlapping consensus, Rawls should have recognized that the "absolute depth" of "irreconcilable latent conflict" (1996, xxvi) among persons renders everything but a *modus vivendi* illegitimate. Rather than worrying about liberal theory being political in the wrong way, Rawls should have recognized that a liberal theory that truly stays on the surface can aspire to nothing greater than endorsement on modus vivendi grounds. This is precisely Richard Rorty's strategy.

Rorty's most recent work in politics is focused on the project of inspiring "social hope" (1999) and "national pride" (1998a). This project, Rorty maintains, involves a decisive turn away from the aspirations of traditional political theory. Rather than arguing for a normative theory of justice or legitimacy, Rorty proposes "inspiring stories" (1998a, 3) which "[clear] philosophy out of the way in order to let the imagination play upon the possibilities of a utopian future" (1999, 239). It is through inspiration, not argumentation, that democratic citizens will come to see themselves as "part of a great human adventure" (1999, 239).

Unlike Rawls, who sees comprehensive liberalism as internally inconsistent, Rorty sees any attempt to justify political practice as a waste of time. He insists that the attempt to ground liberalism is futile because it is couched in an obsolete and naïve philosophical paradigm. According to Rorty, "there is no way to beat [e.g.,] totalitarians in argument by appealing to shared common premises, and no point in pretending that [e.g.,] a common human nature makes the totalitarians unconsciously hold such premises" (1987, 42). Rorty further charges that "attempts to ground a practice on something outside the practice will always be more or less disingenuous" (1996, 333). The lesson we must learn from the failure of the Enlightenment is that "human beings are historical all the way through" (1988, 176), that there are no external facts about human nature, rationality, or morality which supply a foundational premise. Accordingly, any proposed foundation for liberalism will inevitably be "just a hypostatization of certain selected components" of existing democratic practice (1996, 333–334). Rorty writes,

> To say that a certain course of conduct is more in accord with human nature or our moral sense, or more rational, than another is just a fancy way of commending one's own sense of what is most worth preserving in our present practices, of commending our own utopian vision of our community. (1996, 334)

According to Rorty, we must abandon the project of philosophical justification altogether. The antifoundationalist liberal instead offers an attractive "idealization" (1996, 333) of liberalism. He "makes one feature of our culture look good by citing still another," and unabashedly compares our culture with others "by reference to our own standards" (1989, 57). By promoting his politics in this way, the antifoundationalist does not provide a foundation (albeit a relativist one) for his practices, he is not supplying "philosophical backup" for those aspects of his community that he most admires. Rather, he is "putting politics first and tailoring a philosophy to suit" (1988, 178).

Hence, the priority of democracy to philosophy. The antifoundationalist recognizes that a compelling idealization of liberalism is "the only sort of justification we are going to get" (1989, 57). Rorty does not lament this, however. He insists that the purposes of liberal democracy are better served by the antifoundationalist strategy. Rorty claims that "the search for foundations of democracy" is a "distraction from debates between competing idealizations of current practices" (1996, 335).

Rorty's many critics have charged that his account is relativist, irrationalist, emotivist, ethnocentric, self-defeating, and nonprogressive.[14] Rorty is not bothered by such criticisms; he insists that such labels will offend only those who are still practicing the kind of philosophy he has abandoned. For example, to the charge that his antifoundationalism is irrationalist and emotivist, Rorty responds that only those who accept an archaic moral psychology—namely, one that "distinguishes between reason and the passions"—could make such a charge (1996, 334). Similarly, to the suggestion that his account is ethnocentric, Rorty responds that it is because "the philosophical tradition has accustomed us to the idea that anybody who is willing to listen to reason—to hear out all arguments—can be brought around to the truth" that one worries about "ethnocentrism" in political philosophy (1988, 188). The recommendation is to reject this philosophical fantasy.

A different kind of argumentative strategy is required. Let us begin with three central ideas to which Rorty is committed:

1. One cannot achieve a proof of liberalism of the sort the foundationalist wants.
2. Once the foundationalist project is abandoned, all that is left for political philosophy is the enterprise of telling inspiring stories that recommend liberal current practices.
3. Liberal democracy is best served by antifoundationalism.

What Rorty has not explicitly shown is that the only alternative to the Enlightenment dream of a deductive science of politics is his brand of hopeful antifoundationalism. In other words, why should we accept idea two? Rorty's idea two is derived from the consideration that "It is not clear how to argue for the claim that human beings ought to be liberals rather than fanatics without being driven back on a theory of human nature" (1988, 190). Rorty insists that every foundationalist argument will necessarily require something like a theory of human nature for its ground. Again, in order to serve the foundationalist's dialectical purposes, this theory must be external to and independent of any existing social practices; the ground must be ahistorical and metaphysical.

The problem with being driven back upon a theory of human nature is not, as Rawls contends, that consensus on any such theory is unattainable; rather, Rorty objects to the philosophical content itself. He claims that "humanity no more has a nature . . . independent of the accidents of history, than life has a nature independent of the accidents of biological evolution" (1996, 334). There is ultimately no argumentative wall upon which to rely for a proof of democracy. Any proposed wall will turn out to be "a painted backdrop, one more work of man, one more bit of cultural stage-setting" (1989, 53). Rorty's position seems to run as follows:

1. The attempt to get beyond idealizations to foundations will necessarily evoke some theory of human nature.
2. A theory of human nature as something distinct from existing social conditions is incoherent because there is no human nature in this sense.
3. As there is no point external to the contingencies of our society from which to launch a political philosophy, all political philosophy can be is the exercise of promoting various idealizations of current social practices.
4. Therefore, there are only idealizations and no foundations.

The force of this line of reasoning derives entirely from premise two. Why should one accept this premise? Once it is noted that Rorty's support for premise two is his reading of the philosophical implications of Darwin

(1996, 334), the argument collapses. Rorty's second premise rests upon a controversial theory about theories of human nature that is based upon a controversial reading of the philosophical implications of the theory of evolution. One might accuse Rorty of using his controversial reading of Darwin to provide the ground for his antifoundationalist political philosophy. In other words, one might accuse Rorty of arguing the following:

1. Darwin has shown us that life does not have a nature independent of "the accidents of biological evolution."
2. "Human history is simply biological evolution continued by other means" (Rorty 1996, 334).
3. Therefore, there is no human nature apart from "the accidents of history"; human nature is contingent.
4. Therefore, any argument that appeals to some noncontingent sense of human nature is incoherent.
5. By definition, all foundationalist arguments appeal to a noncontingent sense of human nature.
6. Therefore, every foundationalist argument is incoherent and unacceptable.

Here, the crucial premise is the intermediary conclusion three, which supposedly follows from premises one and two. However, premise two involves a speculative, perhaps esoteric, extrapolation from Darwin. Rorty has, therefore, failed to "get along without philosophical presuppositions" (1988, 179); his argument rests upon his own philosophical account of the metaphysical implications of the theory of evolution.

Rorty will undoubtedly resist this reading of his position. He will deny that his antifoundationalist political philosophy rests upon a foundationalist argument from Darwinian biology. In anticipation of this kind of criticism, Rorty writes,

> I am not . . . saying that the . . . account of language and . . . selfhood which I have sketched provide "philosophical foundations of democracy." For the notion of a "philosophical foundation" goes when the vocabulary of Enlightenment rationalism goes. (1989, 44)

However, it is not enough for Rorty to simply announce that he has not employed a foundation—for the issue is not simply terminological—Rorty must show that his reading of Darwin does not function as a foundational premise. That is, he must show that there is a way to run his argument without the implication from premises one and two to premise three. He does not do this.

Moreover, Rorty cannot claim to be following Rawls's program of drawing "solely upon basic intuitive ideas that are embedded in the political institutions of a constitutional democratic regime" (Rawls 1985, 390).[15] The claim that "Human history is simply biological evolution continued by other means" (1996, 334) *is not* a basic intuitive idea operative within our political culture.

Rorty may elect to respond that he has not *argued* for any antifoundationalist conclusion, but rather has simply tried to *persuade* us that,

> For purposes of social theory, we can put aside such topics as an ahistorical human nature, the nature of selfhood, the motive of moral behavior, and the meaning of human life. We treat these as irrelevant to politics as Jefferson thought questions about the Trinity and about transubstantiation. (1988, 180)

Rorty may respond to my argument by simply changing the subject (1989, 44); he might shift from philosophical arguments about the impossibility of escaping contingency to pragmatic talk about how he thinks we might improve politics. In this way, his antifoundationalism consists of nothing more than the attempt to "deflect attention from all questions other than 'what sort of compromise might we be able to freely agree upon?'" (1998b, 120). Rorty's liberalism is thus not properly a liberal theory at all, but rather a plea for doing politics without engaging what Bruce Ackerman (1989, 361) has called "big questions."

An antifoundationalist politics is thus an antiphilosophical politics; accordingly, Rorty is not proposing a political philosophy but proffering liberal propaganda. Rorty's shift from an argument about inescapable contingency to pragmatic preaching will be a strictly tactical—a purely dialectical maneuver designed to end the discussion with his views intact—unless it is accompanied by the recognition that the attitude of the antifoundationalist liberal toward "big questions" is itself contingent. To deny this is to claim that political antifoundationalsim is what Rorty calls a "final vocabulary," a way of describing things that "puts all doubts to rest" (1989, 74), what I shall call a "big answer." But the antifoundationalist is someone who "has radical and continuing doubts" about his own vocabulary, his own way of describing things (Rorty 1989, 73). Antifoundationalists can take no vocabulary to be final, not even the vocabulary of antifoundationalist liberalism. As Rorty says, "we treat everything—our language, our conscience, our community—as a product of time and chance" (1989, 22).

Once the antifoundationalist acknowledges that everything is contingent, he must concede that his antifoundationalist liberalism is tentative. The "big questions" regarding whether democracy can be given foundations, whether there is an ahistorical human nature, and whether reason has a structure, remain open questions. The antifoundationalist cannot adopt the position that Rorty's champions of contingency—Kuhn,

Davidson, Wittgenstein, Nietzsche, Sellars, Feyerabend—have found the "big answers" and thus have had the last word on questions of language, self, society, and science. He cannot rule out *a priori* that, for example, Aristotelian physics, or Kantian Ethics, or Millian philosophy of science is true in a philosophically robust sense of that term, for his rejection of robust senses of true is yet another contingency. In other words, unless he is to appeal to a philosophical proof of antifoundationalism, he must admit that his positions about contingency, foundations, liberalism, and other 'big questions" are not "big answers," and thus are not final.

Rorty will insist that his commitment to contingency implies nothing beyond itself. The idea of a view having further entailments is just one more fiction of the kind of philosophy he no longer is doing. Hence, the only recourse is to engage his claim that democracy is best served by an antifoundationalist vocabulary and self-image. I shall argue not only that Rorty's view is insufficient to deal with certain political realities which currently threaten contemporary democracy, but also that it is unable to inspire the kind of social hope that Rorty takes to be the principal objective of political theory.

Rorty understands philosophical debates among liberals as dialectical competitions between different idealizations of existing social practices. Rorty thinks of the difference between Rawls and Nozick in these terms. We may agree with Rorty that the dispute between Rawls and Nozick really is just a dispute about how we should prioritize our practices. On Rorty's view, Nozick and Rawls simply offer different "intuition pumps" (1996, 333).

However, this suggestion makes sense only if we restrict our analyses to congenial disputes between professional academics such as Rawls and Nozick. The picture breaks down when we consider the more fundamental disputes that arise outside the academy. Consider, for example, Stalin's claim that his brutal regime is democratic "in a higher sense." Does it make sense to say that Stalinism is just another idealization of democracy? The obvious response, one that Rorty would endorse (Rorty 1998a, 57–58), is that Stalinist democracy is not democracy at all. However, it is unclear how Rorty can make the distinction between real democracy and tyranny disguised as democracy while remaining faithful to his antifoundationalism.

Perhaps Rorty would like to treat Stalin as he would treat Nietzsche and Loyola. That is, perhaps he will avoid having to distinguish "real" democracy from tyranny by simply dismissing Stalin as "mad." Of course, on Rorty's view, to call Stalin "mad" is not to render a psychological diagnosis, but simply to say that "there is no way to see [him] as [a] fellow [citizen] of our constitutional democracy"; Rorty thinks Stalin is "crazy" because "the limits of sanity are set by *what we can* take seriously." These limits are, of course, "determined by our upbringing, our historical situation" (1988, 187–188).

This "ethnocentric" (1988, 188) strategy founders once we consider cases of fellow citizens who promote idealizations of our democracy which are similar to those proffered by Stalin, or Hitler, or any of Rorty's other paradigmatic madmen. Members of white-supremacist, or other racist organizations, certainly promote a certain vision of the "utopian future of our community" (1996, 333), a particular image of what is best in our culture. We cannot treat racists as "mad" *and maintain* that "the limits of sanity" are set by the contingencies of community, for, in this case, the "madmen" *are members* of my community; the KKK is as much a part of my liberal inheritance as the ACLU and the AFL-CIO. Rorty must either introduce some *ad hoc* qualifications to the terms ethnocentrism, idealization, and social practice, such that racists will necessarily not count as one of us, or he will have to concede that the modern democratic state is home to persons who promote views that differ substantially from his own. He must acknowledge that when he writes sentences like, "For purposes of social theory, we can put aside such topics as an ahistorical human nature, the nature of selfhood, the motive of moral behavior, and the meaning of human life" (1988, 180), the pronoun "we" actually refers to a very small sector of the democratic community. In fact, citizens of the United States very often think that "big questions" matter for politics, and many of our political commitments are determined by the answers we favor.

Given these political realities, we simply cannot afford to treat philosophical disputes about politics in the way that Rorty recommends; there is much more at stake in some disputes than idealizations. We must face the fact that, in the interests of the kind of open discussion that is requisite to self-government, a democratic regime allows an extremely wide variety of political organizations to operate. Some of these agencies aim to use democracy to undermine democracy. That is, some use the openness of democracy to propagate supposedly "big answers" which are not only false, but inimical to democracy. Concerning Rorty's view, we would have to treat these as alternative intuition pumps and hope for the best. Meanwhile, as Seyla Benhabib, among many others, notes, there is evidence which suggests that in recent years "even in the United States" neofascist organizations "have emerged on a scale unprecedented since the end of World War II" (Benhabib 1996, 3).[16]

Rorty's antifoundationalism leaves us impotent to respond to such threats; he suggests that, when dealing with opponents of democracy, we "ask [them] to privatize their projects" (1989, 197). And what shall we do when they refuse? We simply change the subject or cut the conversation short; Rorty recommends that we simply "refuse to argue" with them (1988, 190).

Against this strategy, Robert Dahl has raised the following considerations:

> [L]et us imagine a country with democratic political institutions in which intellectual elites are in the main convinced that democracy cannot be justified on reasonable and plausible grounds. The prevailing view among them, let us suppose, is that no intellectually respectable reasons exist for believing that a democratic system is better than a nondemocratic alternative. As long as the political, social, and economic institutions of the country are performing adequately from the perspective of the general population, perhaps most people will simply ignore the querulous dissent of their intellectuals; and political leaders and influential opinion makers may in the main go along with the generally favorable popular view. But in time of serious crisis—and all countries go through time of serious crisis—those who try to defend democracy will find the going much harder, while those who promote nondemocratic alternatives will find it that much easier. (1996, 338)

Rorty's strategy of dismissing democracy's enemies rather than attempting to engage them is likely to strengthen the antidemocratic tendencies that are already operative within our society, and thus might even help to precipitate the kind of crisis that Dahl describes. Here it is important to note that the antidemocratic forces operatives within our society do propose philosophical arguments in favor of their views, and they believe that they have good reasons to hold the positions they do.[17]

We may draw this discussion to a close by noting that Rorty's political antifoundationalism places liberal democracy on a philosophical par with tyranny. There is, Rorty insists, nothing one can say against tyranny that should count as a good reason for the tyrant to become a democrat. Rorty further contends that giving up the Enlightenment illusion that tyrants can somehow be refuted will improve existing democracies. Once political theorists give up the "distraction" (1996, 133) of trying to develop foundations for democracy, they can take up their proper work of helping to inspire within democratic citizens the social hope requisite to achieving our country.

The inspired fascination with democracy that Rorty seeks to cultivate is important; however, an essential component of hope is the confidence that what is hoped for is in some relevant way worth achieving and better than the other things that might develop. Yet Rorty does not allow one to maintain that democracy is in any relevant way better than, say, tyranny. Hence, Rorty's social hope must be ironic—we must hope to achieve that which we no longer can think is worth achieving, we must draw inspiration from that which we contend is essentially not inspiring. If there is anything inspiring in the works of Rorty's heroes, such as Whitman and Dewey, it is precisely the sense that the visions of democracy they present are in a nonironic sense worth trying for and worth hoping to achieve. This can be maintained only if one can point to some aspect of democracy that relevantly distinguishes it from tyranny.

If these arguments are correct, then neither Rawlsian political liberalism, nor Galstonian liberal pluralism, nor Rortyian antifoundationalism, successfully allay the tension within liberal theory. This leaves us with the option either to return to a roughly traditional comprehensive liberal theory and deal with the difficulties I raised in the previous chapter,[18] or seek a new kind of political theory. In the chapters that follow, I shall draw upon pragmatist, deliberative democratic, and civic republican sources in taking the latter route.

CHAPTER 5

The Deliberative Turn in Democratic Theory

It may seem that I have said very little about democracy; however, democracy has been implicitly the subject of the entire discussion. Now it is time to bring democracy to the fore and to make explicit the connection between liberalism and democracy. Specifically, we shall discover what the failure of liberal theory means for democratic politics and why a theory of democracy that is "after liberalism" is necessary.

Liberalism and the Democratic Predicament

Early in Book VI of Plato's *Republic*, Socrates presents a powerful challenge to democracy in the form of an image of an imperiled ship (488a–489d).[1] The shipowner—here representative of the *demos*—is at once the most powerful force on board but also the most easily confused. Surrounded by sailors eager to gain control of the ship, the owner is constantly bombarded with suggestions, advice, and exhortations designed to persuade him to relinquish the helm. The owner is eventually stupefied and bewildered by these pleas and turns his rudder over to the sailors. As the sailors know nothing about navigation and seek only private advantage, each wants to take the ship in a different direction. The sailors, therefore, compete with each other for control; mayhem ensues, leaving the ship without a coherent plan. Meanwhile, the "true captain"—the analogue of the philosopher—who does not seek control of the ship, but wants only to understand "all that pertains to his craft" (488d) is derided, censured, and thought a "useless stargazer" (489c) by everyone on board. Surely, a ship directed by those who know nothing of navigation cannot hope to find its proper port.

The lesson of the story is that "The best among the philosophers are useless to the majority" (489b). Since a democratic city is one which is ruled by the many (557a),[2] the philosophers, the true "knowers" who are few in number, have no place in a democracy. As the many are "hard of hearing," "short-sighted," and "intellectually deficient" (488b); they are easily swayed by the rhetoric of sophists and politicians who seek political power for private advantage and who know nothing about justice. The democratic city is destined to founder.

Accordingly, Socrates is wary of democracy. A city that has no concern for knowledge and wisdom cannot be just and stable. Socrates accepts the premise that it is the purpose of a just city to promote the good life among persons. As the task of promoting the good life requires knowledge of what is good, political power in the just city should be distributed according to one's knowledge about goodness. Since the knowledge that philosophy pursues is knowledge of what is good, political power properly belongs to the philosopher alone.[3] In a just city, then, political power is invested entirely in a special class of philosophers, which Socrates calls the "guardians" (412c ff.). Consequently, democracy is among the worst forms of political association; as it invests political power in the foolish many, it is unable to achieve the purpose of politics and is, therefore, unjust.[4]

Borrowing a term from Robert Dahl (1989, Ch. 4–5), we may refer to Socrates' challenge to democracy as the "Guardianship Argument." Updating the vocabulary a bit, we can pose the argument as follows.

The Guardianship Argument

1. The just city promotes the good life among its citizens.
2. There is a special kind of knowledge, which we shall call "political knowledge," which gives its possessor the knowledge necessary to the effective promotion of the good life among citizens. A person who has this kind of knowledge possesses "political wisdom."
3. Therefore, political power ought to be distributed according to political wisdom.
4. Political wisdom is not equally distributed among persons; rather, some are politically wise and some are not.
5. Therefore, political power should not be equally distributed; those possessing political wisdom should wield the political power, whereas those lacking political wisdom should have none.

That this line of reasoning constitutes an objection to democracy should be clear: Insofar as it establishes that political power should not be distributed among citizens equally, but invested entirely in a class of "guardians," it recommends an antidemocratic political arrangement.[5] Although the Guardianship Argument presumes many substantive philosophical principles, it is especially important to focus on two key claims presumed by the argument.[6] We call the first the "Political Wisdom Principle":

Political Wisdom Principle: (1) Normative claims about politics are cognitive, and (2) knowledge of the truth values of normative political claims (i.e., political wisdom) is possible.

We shall refer to the first part of the Political Wisdom Principle as the "cognitivity claim," and to the second part as the "knowability claim." Additionally, the Guardianship Argument rests upon a second principle, which we refer to as the "Epistemarchy Principle":[7]

Epistemarchy Principle: Political wisdom entitles the politically wise person to a share of political power directly proportionate to his wisdom. Conversely, those lacking political wisdom should lack political power.

One can understand the tradition of liberal philosophy as a series of attempts to respond to the Guardianship Argument by rejecting at least one of these principles. The varieties of comprehensive liberalism, with the exception of Mill's theory, deny the Epistemarchy Principle.[8] The liberal idea of political rights, as employed by Locke, Kant, and the early Rawls, establishes that political participation is not contingent upon individual political wisdom. If it is true that each of us "possesses an inviolability . . . that even the welfare of society as a whole cannot override" (TJ, 3), then political rights, the formal statements of individual inviolability, are what Ronald Dworkin famously has called "trump cards" (Dworkin 1978, 198). If each person has rights, and if these rights entitle each person to equal treatment and political participation, then the absolute wisdom of Socrates' ideal philosopher does not justify philosophical kingship.

To recall the results of the foregoing, the force of this kind of response to the Guardianship Argument rests upon the strength of the philosophical theory of individual rights it presupposes. As we have seen, the project of grounding liberalism in a comprehensive philosophical theory is fraught with difficulty; any robust philosophical account of individual rights will presuppose, imply, or favor what Rawls has called, in his later work, a "comprehensive doctrine" about which well-intentioned and sincere persons may reasonably disagree. However, one of the basic commitments of liberalism is that the state should be neutral and impartial with regard to deep philosophical theories concerning human nature and the good life. Therefore, it appears that the project of comprehensive liberalism, the project of providing a deep philosophical theory to ground a politics that attempts to eschew deep philosophical commitments, may be, as one critic has said, an "oxymoronic conundrum" (Barber 1998b, 3).

In response to the failure of the comprehensive project, noncomprehensive theories have targeted the Political Wisdom Principle. Specifically, the political liberal abstains from comment on the cognitivity claim (Rawls 1996, 128) and denies the knowability claim.[9] That denial is implied by the fact of reasonable pluralism. If it is not the case that all rational roads lead to a single and specific moral doctrine, then it is the case that nobody can *know* which rational moral doctrines are true. If nobody can *know* which (or if any) moral doctrines are true, then nobody is politically wise in the sense the Guardianship Argument requires. The political liberal concludes that philosopher kings cannot exist because even a fully rational human cannot have the kind of knowledge Socrates envisions.

By contrast, the antifoundationalist liberal explicitly denies both parts of the Political Wisdom Principle. According to the antifoundationalist, political claims, like every other kind of claim, are not cognitive. As Rorty has put it, when "philosophy goes antifoundationalist . . . the question, 'Is there any evidence for *p*?' gets replaced by the question, 'Is there any way of getting a consensus on what would count in favor of *p*?'" (1997, 155). Since normative political claims have no truth value, there is no political knowledge, and therefore, no political wisdom. Platonic kings cannot exist because the kind of knowledge they are supposed to have does not exist.

Liberal Democracy and Its Discontents

Despite variations in their logical details, liberal attempts to diffuse the Guardianship Argument exhibit the common strategy of divorcing politics from Socrates' concerns about truth, knowledge, and goodness. The kernel of Socrates' objection to democracy is that a democratic arrangement cannot give the appropriate degree of authority to knowledge and those who possess it. Liberals have promoted a vision of politics according to which, the best a state can do to promote the good life among its citizens is to leave substantive questions of the good life out of politics. The liberal state, therefore, seeks not to cultivate virtue or impose truth, but to establish and maintain the social conditions under which individuals can "take charge of their lives" (Rawls 1996, 189) and pursue their "own good in [their] own way" (Mill 1859, 17).

The liberal image of free and equal individuals, pursuing their own conceptions of the good, suggests a particular vision of democratic politics. While liberal individuals are busy pursuing their own goods in their own ways, business that is properly called "political" must be conducted: Laws must be enacted, policies must be instituted, resources must be allocated, and public decisions must be made. These decisions and policies will inevitably impact individual lives; and these effects will not always be consonant with the immediate interests of all.[10] As the liberal has denied that politics must aim at the Platonic ideals of Wisdom, Goodness, and Justice, there is no political *telos* apart from the satisfaction of individual interests, understood strictly as preferences. Since preferences conflict, what is required is a political process that can fairly decide public policy. On the liberal view, then, democratic processes are essentially instruments by which the competing preferences of distinct, independent, and self-interested agents may be aggregated fairly. The paradigmatically political act, according to the liberal, is that of registering one's preferences in an official procedure where each individual counts for one, and no individual counts for more than one. Hence, Jane Mansbridge characterizes liberal democracy as "adversary democracy":

> Voters pursue their individual interests by making demands on the political system in proportion to the intensity of their feelings. Politicians, also pursuing their own interests, adopt policies that buy them votes, thus ensuring accountability. In order to stay in office, politicians act like entrepreneurs and brokers, looking for formulas that satisfy as many, and alienate as few, interests as possible. From the interchange between self-interested voters and self-interested brokers, emerge decisions that come as close as possible to a balanced aggregation of individual interests. (1983, 17)

Jürgen Habermas has recently offered a similar description,

> According to the 'liberal' or Lockean view, the democratic process accomplishes the task of programming the government in the interest of society where the government is represented as an apparatus of public administration, and society as a market-structured network of interactions among private persons. (1996, 21)

Habermas further states that, on the liberal view of democracy, political rights "such as voting rights and free speech" serve the purpose of providing citizens "the opportunity to assert their private interests in such a way that . . . these interests are finally aggregated into a political will that makes an impact on the administration" (1996, 22).[11] Iris Young has nicely summarized the liberal/aggregative view as follows:

> The aggregative model describes democratic processes of policy formation something like this. Individuals in the polity have varying preferences about what they want government institutions to do.

They know that other individuals also have preferences, which may or may not match their own. Democracy is a competitive process in which political parties and candidates offer their platforms and attempt to satisfy the largest number of people's preferences. Citizens with similar preferences often organize interest groups in order to influence the actions of parties and policy-makers, once they are elected.

Individuals, interest-groups, and public officials each may behave strategically, adjusting the orientation of their pressure tactics or coalition-building according to their perceptions of the activities of competing preferences. Assuming the process of competition, strategizing, coalition-building, and responding to pressure is open and fair, the outcome of both elections and legislative decisions reflects the aggregation of the strongest or most widely held preferences in the population. (2000, 19)

What makes this aggregative account distinctively liberal is that the political will, which emerges from the democratic/aggregative process, is constrained by the liberal principles. In this way, the individual is, on the one hand, protected *by* democracy from the oppression of tyrants and, on the other hand, protected *from* democracy by the rights and entitlements bestowed upon the individual by liberalism. In other words, liberal democracy renders all forms of nonpopular rule illegitimate and establishes a network of constraints on the political will, which protects individuals from what Tocqueville famously called the "tyranny of the majority" (1835, 722–731).

As its objectives are exclusively protective, a liberal democracy is essentially a kind of *state*. Accordingly, liberal theorists tend to focus upon issues concerning the political apparatus and institutions by which private interests and preferences are managed. On this view, democracy resides in the formal procedures by which public policy is decided and enacted; voting in popular elections and referenda, opinion polling and other means of communication between citizens and their representatives, distributions of power within government structures, and the like. Once the appropriate procedural apparatus is in place, democracy is established.

A political theory that construes politics as a matter of fairly aggregating the competing interests of free and equal individuals is certainly an effective solvent of monarchic, aristocratic, oligarchic, and theocratic arrangements. Liberalism has thus enjoyed a successful relationship with democracy since Locke's liberal defense of the Whig Revolution of 1688 in his *Second Treatise*. It is important to recognize that liberal democracy arose out of and, in response to, specific historical conditions. We shall see that the conditions which gave rise to liberal democracy no longer prevail, and that liberal democracy is unable to address and deal effectively with current conditions.

Liberalism, along with its distinctive vision of democracy, was originally posed as a revolutionary philosophy. Like any philosophy of revolution, liberalism was formulated with a particular target in view. Specifically, liberalism is a reaction against monarchy and aristocracy. Accordingly, Jefferson's *Declaration*, a revolutionary document if there ever was one, begins with a concise yet powerful affirmation of liberalism. However, whereas liberalism criticized the entrenched power of monarchs and aristocrats, it overlooked—in fact, it depended upon and presupposed—the philosophical, moral, and theological social homogeneity which monarchy and aristocracy generate. In other words, the stability of a monarchy or an aristocracy depends, in large measure, upon the ability of the ruling element to instill among the ruled classes what Rawls has called a comprehensive doctrine, a systematic set of moral, theological, and philosophical beliefs and commitments. Specifically, a monarch, for example, must impose upon his subjects a comprehensive view according to which the rule of kings is just. Historically, monarchy relied upon a comprehensive view that kings were selected by God, and therefore, were possessed of divine authority.[12] Insofar as the king could instill this view among his subjects and discourage or suppress dissenting and conflicting doctrines, his rule was relatively stable.

Although a king can be dethroned in the course of a revolution, the common comprehensive doctrine his regime imposed upon his subjects cannot. The moral and theological commitments, along with their social manifestations, remain long after the king is dead; they reside in the habits, attitudes, and customs of his former subjects. It is precisely the social homogeneity produced by monarchic and aristocratic regimes that traditional liberals unwittingly took for granted in developing their comprehensive liberal theories. This is why, for example, Locke sees nothing particularly illiberal in his recommendation regarding the treatment of "those who deny the being of a God" (1689b, 313). To the seventeenth-century Englishman, atheists were barbaric outsiders unfit for civil society—the recently dethroned king assured him that the only way to survive in the society from which Locke's liberal democracy was supposed to emerge was to assert the existence of God.

Further, the moral, theological, and philosophical homogeneity that was presupposed by comprehensive liberalism also informed the aggregative conception of democracy. The very idea that processes of opinion aggregation by which majorities rule (albeit within certain constraints) can give rise to a political will, which accurately represents the public good and hence constitutes self-government, presupposes the existence of shared commitments and ideals among otherwise distinct and independent individuals; at the very least, it presupposes a shared commitment among individuals to the democratic process itself. Moreover, that traditional theorists of liberal democracy pay so little attention to the concerns raised by Socrates' foundering ship regarding the vulnerability of the populace to demagoguery and other forms of manipulation, suggests a confidence among the theorists in the intellectual powers of individuals, which is warranted only if an elaborate system of education is presupposed.

In short, traditional liberal theorists unwittingly appealed to the social conditions established by the regimes they sought to overthrow for the foundations of their liberalism. For as long as the residual social homogeneity prevailed and remained influential, liberal democracy succeeded as a political doctrine. However, with time the common ground established by the monarchs and aristocrats receded, and the foundations of comprehensive liberalism began to erode. Advances in technology led to increased communication, trade, and influence among diverse peoples; accordingly, the region of tacit agreement on political essentials within a particular society shrank, and the realm of explicit difference expanded. Hence, as our study has shown, the tradition of liberal philosophy exhibits a gradual but steady retreat from thick philosophical foundations.

In contemporary times, democratic states are marked not by shared commitments and common ground, but by distance, disagreement, and difference. Theorists of liberal democracy, hence, find themselves in the Rawlsian conundrum upon which this study has been focused: How can a liberal democratic society propose a philosophical account of its practices and institutions that is adequately robust to answer antidemocrats and sufficiently inclusive to win the assent of citizens who disagree about philosophical, moral, and theological essentials? In the absence of a philosophically robust account, liberal democrats find themselves unable to say why liberal democracy is more just than, and preferable to, mild oligarchy or benevolent dictatorship. Moreover, the lack of a philosophical account of liberal democracy causes the corresponding lack of a theory of citizenship, a reasoned account of what self-government and civic participation consist in, and why they are important. Liberals who take up the challenge of formulating the requisite philosophical accounts will confront the endemic tension in liberalism. Given that modern democratic states are marked by a pervasive social pluralism, any robust theory of democracy will inevitably conflict with some reasonable comprehensive doctrines and favor others; any such theory will violate the liberal commitment to political neutrality.

Theorists of liberal democracy traditionally have tried to do without a theory of citizenship and civic participation. Again, insofar as a shared sense of purpose and responsibility developed from other sources, such as the family, the community, the civic association, the public school, the local church, and the trade union, liberal democracy did not need a theory of citizenship. Moreover, the aggregative conception of democracy, focused as it is upon private preferences and individual strategizing, renders the very idea of citizenship superfluous to self-government. We now live at a time in which all of the aforementioned institutions, among many others, are in decline. Political participation and civic mindedness are also declining; meanwhile, public ignorance, citizen incompetence, and distrust of government are on the rise.[13] As theorists of liberal democracy are caught in the dilemma between philosophical foundations and political neutrality, they are powerless to address the challenges to democracy that social pluralism involves. As Benjamin Barber has said, "Liberalism . . . is far more suited to founding than to sustaining democracy" (1998b, 31).

The Deliberative Turn

Recently, antiliberal political theorists have sought to formulate the intellectual tools with which to rehabilitate American democracy. The principal step in this rehabilitation is the overcoming of the aggregative, adversarial conception of democracy. Drawing upon Robert Putnam's (1993) fascinating and influential study of emerging democracy in the southern regions of Italy and related work, these theorists have argued that, in the absence of complex cultural and civic networks of cooperation and engagement, what Putnam calls "social capital" (1993, 167), democracy simply does not work. The traditional view of the liberal democrats that democracy is essentially a kind of *state*, a collection of formal procedures and institutions, is false. Antiliberal democratic theorists have thus called for a rejection of liberalism's image of the independent, autonomous individual that harbors fixed preferences and a return to community, civil society, voluntarism, belonging, participation, and the virtues requisite to self-government.[14]

The collectivist rhetoric of democratic antiliberalism has understandably generated suspicion and apprehension among liberals. The plea for a return to community values, civic virtue (Sandel 1996, 25), and a common "moral voice" (Etzioni 1993, 12) evokes worries of oppression, majoritarianism, discrimination, and conformity. Certainly, many of the most morally horrendous episodes in human history have occurred with community support. As one liberal critic has put it, "The enforcement of liberal rights, not the absence of settled community, stands between the Moral Majority and the contemporary equivalent of witch hunting" (Gutmann 1985, 132–133).

I shall not review the details of the so-called "liberal-communitarian debate."[15] It is worth noting, however, that parties on both sides have begun to supplement their views with an admission of the need to include, within democratic theory, an account of public discourse, debate, and deliberation. Liberal thinkers such as John Rawls, Amy Gutmann, Dennis Thompson, Joshua Cohen, and Bruce Ackerman have emphasized the role of "public reason" and deliberation in democratic decision making.[16] Antiliberal thinkers, including Michael Sandel, Iris Young, Seyla Benhabib, and Benjamin Barber have similarly promoted a conception of democracy in which public discussion and cooperative, participatory discourse are central.[17] Hence a vast literature on "deliberative democracy" has emerged recently.[18]

Despite this apparent convergence of otherwise divided theorists upon the need for deliberation, the particular theories of deliberative democracy tend to divide neatly according to liberal/antiliberal lines.[19] However, as I presently shall argue, neither style of deliberative theory is satisfactory. Exposing the limitations of the different accounts of democratic deliberation will help us to discern what a satisfactory theory would look like.

Liberal Deliberativism

Contemporary theorists of liberalism seek to mitigate the dissociative and deracinating tendencies of the adversarial model[20] offered by traditional liberals by promoting an "ideal of democratic citizenship" (Rawls 1996, 217) in which citizens come together in a "public political forum" (Rawls 1999b, 133). A realm in which "free public reason among equals" (Cohen 1996, 412) can operate. Within this realm,

> participants regard one another as equals. They aim to defend and criticize institutions and programs in terms of considerations that others have reason to accept, given the fact of reasonable pluralism and the assumption that those others are reasonable; and they are prepared to cooperate in accordance with the results of such discussion, treating those results as authoritative. (Cohen 1996, 413; cf. Rawls 1996, 218)

Cohen's invocation of reasonable pluralism is important. It is a fundamental feature of liberal deliberation theories that public reason be engaged under a specific set of restraints and restrictions. Particularly, liberal theorists of deliberative democracy tend to assert that the fact of reasonable pluralism constrains public reason, with respect to the kinds of reasons that can be employed in public debate. On the liberal view, one must avoid introducing reasons that presuppose or draw from one's own comprehensive doctrine. When deliberating, citizens must confine themselves to considerations that others have reason to accept; reasons that derive from a particular comprehensive doctrine cannot win general acceptance in public debate, and are therefore, inadmissible.

On the liberal view, then, citizens must conduct public debate in strictly political terms. Consequently, the liberal places restriction not only upon the reasons deliberating citizens can employ in public debate, but also upon the questions which are suitable for the public deliberative agenda. Questions and issues that cannot be debated in political terms are removed from the political agenda. Rawls explains, "Faced with the fact of reasonable pluralism, a liberal view removes from the political agenda the most divisive issues, serious contention about which must undermine the bases of social cooperation" (1996, 157). Thomas Nagel concurs,

> Where no common standpoint is available at any level to authorize the collective determination by democratic procedures of policies about which individuals find themselves in radical disagreement because of incompatible values, it is best, if possible, to remove those subjects from the reach of political action. (1991, 166)

Therefore, liberal democratic deliberation is subject to what Bruce Ackerman calls "conversational restraints" (1989, 16):

> When you and I learn that we disagree about a dimension of the moral truth, we should not search for some common value that will trump this disagreement . . . we should simply say nothing at all about this disagreement and try to solve our problem by invoking premises that we do agree upon. In restraining ourselves in this way, we need not lose the chance to talk to one another about our deepest moral disagreements in countless other, more private, contexts. (1989, 16–17)

Ackerman's term, "conversational restraint," is especially apt because it captures the dual aspect of the constraint. Liberal deliberation conversation is restrained with respect to one's reasons and with respect to the topics which can be deliberated about. As public debate must be conducted in terms that others "have reason to accept" (Cohen 1996, 413), it must eschew deep controversy at the level of comprehensive doctrines. Consequently, attempts to settle deep moral, religious, and philosophical disputes are removed from politics and relegated to the private realm.

As is suggested by the previous quotations, liberals advocate public discussion and debate, yet place the basic commitments and principles of liberalism beyond the reach of political deliberation. Gutmann and

Thompson are explicit on this point; they write, "Even in deliberative democracy, deliberation does not have priority over liberty and opportunity." Regarding their view, basic liberty and fair opportunity are "constraints on what counts as a morally legitimate resolution of disagreement" (1996, 17). They are "partly independent" values (1996, 366, n. 18).

What is troubling about this conception of deliberation is that the constraints placed upon deliberation are themselves not generated by the kind of public deliberative processes the liberals advocate. Theorists, such as Rawls and Cohen, restrict the use of nonpublic reasons in political debate as a matter of course. Despite the fact they identify the need for "free deliberation among equals" as a requirement of the legitimacy of political decisions (Cohen 1989, 72), they seek to *impose* this restriction *ex ante*, without public deliberation. It is in this sense that the constraints represent independent values.

This feature of the liberal theories of deliberation invites an objection, raised by theorists as diverse as James Johnson (1998), Robert George (1999), Stanley Fish (1999), Chantal Mouffe (2000), and Ian Shapiro (2003, 22–26), that liberal deliberative democracy is rigged to favor liberal outcomes. To see this, let us briefly consider the controversy in America regarding abortion. Religious believers tend to oppose abortion on the basis of a comprehensive doctrine according to which human life begins at conception. On a liberal conception of public reason, religious believers could not appeal to this doctrine of the beginning of human life in a public debate; reasons that are couched in a comprehensive doctrine are ipso facto nonpublic and inadmissible in public deliberation. To invoke Ackerman's phrase, such reasons are reserved for and restricted to "other, more private contexts" (1989, 17). If one is to make a public case against abortion, one must avoid appealing to controversial theories of when human life begins, and instead, demonstrate that the political values embedded within our shared political tradition—values which "all citizens as reasonable and rational might reasonably be expected to endorse" (Rawls 1996, 236)—weigh in against abortion. However, to require of citizens that public discussion of important matters be conducted in this attenuated, "political not metaphysical," mode is to beg the very questions that religious opponents of abortion are often trying to engage. The question regarding abortion rights is as much about how political and nonpolitical values should be prioritized, as it is about the protection of the life of unborn persons. Therefore, to introduce into the very conception of public reason a restriction that favors political values such as equality, equal rights to reproductive control, and so forth to other values is to program public deliberation to favor certain outcomes. The liberal constraints on public reason thus seem blatantly unfair to those who believe that certain values—the respect for human life, for instance—should outweigh the liberal political values.[21]

The respect in which liberal deliberation is fixed so as to produce the kinds of outcomes liberals tend to favor is especially evident in Cohen's (1998, 195–197) brief discussion of the recent Papal encyclical, *Evangelium Vitae*. Cohen contrasts the position of those who oppose abortion on the basis of faith or "revealed truths" with the position stated by Pope John Paul II. Quoting the encyclical, Cohen demonstrates that the Pope maintains that the truth of the Catholic view on abortion can be "known in its essential traits by human reason" and that the "Law of God" which forbids abortion is "knowable by reason itself" (1998, 196). The case against abortion promoted by the Pope differs, then, from those based in claims of faith and revealed truths. Whereas as the latter reasons "can be reasonably rejected by others" and therefore "cannot serve to justify legislation" (Cohen 1998, 195), the Pope's case seems to appeal not to a comprehensive doctrine, but to reason itself. Therefore, the Pope's case cannot be dismissed as nonpublic and inappropriate for public deliberation. Rather than engaging the arguments raised by the encyclical, however, Cohen offers the revealing response, "We must show that the conception of reason [the encyclical] appeals to is itself sectarian and that the argument [against abortion] fails on a conception of reason that is not" (1998, 196). Cohen gives no indication of what a "sectarian" conception of reason is, or how it differs from his own, presumably nonsectarian, conception of reason. Nor does he demonstrate that the Pope's argument against abortion indeed fails on a nonsectarian conception of reason. Moreover, he gives no indication of how one would go about demonstrating that a conception of reason is "sectarian."[22] The sense of Cohen's response is nonetheless clear: Reason, properly understood, will not contradict current liberal intuitions about abortion. Antiabortion arguments that make appeals to "reason" covertly involve sectarian principles.

In discussing a similar example, Gutmann and Thompson confidently declare that appeals to religious reasons as the basis for illiberal policies "can be shown to be rationalizations" (1990, 70). Yet, as Fish has argued, such declarations that religious reasons are beyond the pale, is not an argument, but rather a "succession of dismissive gestures" (1999, 91). And Shapiro notes that any fundamentalist "will rightly expect to come out on the short end of any deliberative exchange" conducted in Gutmann and Thompson's terms. Shapiro concludes, "The Gutmann-Thompson model works only for those fundamentalists who also count themselves fallibilist democrats"; he continues, "That, I fear, is an empty class, destined to remain uninhabited" (Shapiro 2003, 26).

In light of these considerations, one can plausibly argue that, despite their ostensible turn from aggregation toward deliberation, liberal theorists of deliberative democracy have retained precisely the element which rendered the adversarial model unsatisfactory, namely, the view that citizens come into the political arena distinct, independent entities with competing and irreconcilable fixed interests. The "conversational restraints" imposed upon public discussion among them serves to divert attention from the "absolute depth" of their "irreconcilable conflict" (Rawls 1996, xxvi). More specifically, the prior restraints liberals impose on public debate establish a framework within which otherwise divided citizens can find and work from common ground. However, liberals cannot give citizens non-question-begging reasons to accept those prior constraints on their public discourse. Why should, for example, a Catholic opponent of abortion accept a conception of public debate that explicitly disqualifies his way of framing and deliberating about the abortion issue? Why should he agree to participate in a deliberative procedure that requires, as a condition of participation (and reasonableness), that he leave his true reasons for opposing abortion unexpressed? William Galston has written,

> It is difficult to imagine that any liberal democracy can sustain conscientious support if it tells millions of its citizens that they cannot rightly say what they believe as part of democratic public dialogue. (1999, 43; cf. Johnson 1998, 167–170)

Liberals will want to respond that the Catholic's way of framing the issue, his very conception of what the abortion question *is*, is derived from his comprehensive doctrine, and therefore, contestable by reasonable persons. Hence, questions about when fully human life begins, and other questions with regard to which there is "no common ground" (Nagel 1991, 166) upon which a decision can be reached, are removed from the agenda of public debate. It is in this way that liberal deliberative theories retain the basic premise of the adversarial model; rather than recommending that citizens try to cooperatively discover or even forge common ground at the deepest levels, the liberals understand deep conflicts to be unresolvable and permanent. Disagreements are thus construed as stark *differences*; differences which cannot be overcome, which are unanalyzable and pervasive. Recognizing that democratic politics requires cooperation at some level, liberals propose a deliberative model that requires citizens to ignore their differences.

Michael Sandel's response here is entirely reasonable: "Whether it is possible to reason our way to agreement on any given moral or political controversy is not something we can know until we try" (1998a, 210–211). We cannot determine *a priori* which of our disagreements stem from irreconcilable differences; accordingly, we cannot establish *a priori* "percepts of reasonable discussion" (Rawls 1989a, 478) with which to constrain public discourse. Moreover, the liberal presumption that all deep philosophical, moral, and theological disagreements cannot be settled through the public use of reason, and hence, should be removed from the public agenda, is itself a controversial claim about which reasonable persons may disagree.

A consistent liberal theorist would, therefore, allow public deliberation itself to determine what should count as "public" reasons. Further, the liberal strategy of placing constraints upon the public deliberative process, which render all debate about the basic commitments of liberalism nonpublic, presumes that current understandings and interpretations of those commitments are final, complete, and beyond revision. However, it is reasonable to expect that liberalism has not yet received its final expression.[23] Again, the liberal strategy presumes that current interpretations and understandings of the principles of liberalism are not themselves subjects of widespread contention. But the interpretation of the basic commitments of liberalism is indeed contentious business! The current literature is rife with disagreement between fellow liberals concerning the precise nature of the liberal commitments to such ideals as equality, liberty, and fair opportunity.[24] Moreover, as Seyla Benhabib notes,

> All struggles against oppression in the modern world begin by redefining what had previously been considered private, nonpublic, and nonpolitical issues as matters of public concern, issues of justice, and sites of power that need discursive legitimation. (1992b, 84)

Liberal deliberativism is thus unsatisfactory. Recognizing the need for a theory of democratic citizenship and participation, liberals turned away from the aggregative/adversarial conception of democracy with which their doctrine has been associated. However, in framing a conception of public deliberation, the liberals wanted to ensure that their basic commitments to equality, liberty, and fairness could not be overridden by or revised in public deliberation. They accordingly promoted a view of deliberation that places disagreements regarding liberal basics permanently off the agenda of public debate. They thereby retained the principal feature of the view they sought to abandon: The idea that political agents are not essentially cooperative participants joining in a shared undertaking, but adversaries, strategic competitors, and combatants. Liberal appeals to public reasons, the percepts of reasonable discussion, and conversational restraints are devices instituted to generate common ground. However, as this common ground depends upon persons agreeing to leave their private doctrines—that is, what they truly believe—out of political discussion, it is artificial, plastic, and fragile.

The liberal deliberativists thus offer an inadequate conception of citizenship. On the liberal view, citizens come together to deliberate, not as equal participants in the shared undertaking of self-government, but essentially as strangers; citizens deliberate not as persons, but as distilled public personae purified of nonpublic conceptions. As Sandel has argued, "On the liberal conception, we respect our fellow citizen's moral and religious convictions by ignoring them" (1998, 217). The liberal conception, therefore, construes democratic participation as a kind of formal performance in which actors portray idealized, but nonetheless fictional, characters scripted to cooperatively reason together. In short, liberals offer a democratic citizenship without any actual engagement between persons. In other words, they offer no conception of democratic citizenship at all.

Antiliberal Deliberativism

Whereas liberals insist that political deliberation avoid moral concepts and controversy, the model of deliberation promoted by antiliberals is obsessed with morality. According to antiliberal deliberative theorists, shared moral discourse among citizens is the means by which a fragmented liberal community may "recover its civic voice" (Sandel 1996, 324). Participation in "public discourse" is the activity by which "*me* language" is transformed into "*we* language" (Barber 1998b, 13). That is, the shared activity of "moral dialogue" restores community values by overcoming differences through an appeal to "overarching values" implicitly shared (Etzioni 1998, 186). Through such dialogue, citizens come "to affirm new, renewed, or some other set of values" (Etzioni 1998, 190). As Barber explains:

> A public voice expressing the civility of a cooperative civil society speaks in terms that reveal and elicit common grounds, cooperative strategies, overlapping interests, and a sense of the public weal. (1998a, 116)

Where liberals tend to construe disagreements among persons as necessarily insurmountable differences which are best removed from the public agenda, the antiliberals are confident that commonality, shared purposes, and overlapping interests underlie all or most political disagreement. That is, while liberals tend to see agreement on fundamental matters as adventitious, artificial, and at best transitory,[25] the antiliberals take disagreement as inauthentic and temporary; they maintain that beneath the dissonance of public disagreement and conflict there is a latent harmony of purposes and interests. Public deliberation is the process by which this deep agreement, suppressed by liberal politics, can surface and come to flourish. The value of deliberation hence lies in its power to realize the immanent sense of community among seemingly divided persons.

Although the antiliberals promote an optimistic, and even gratifying, picture of human society, there are many problems with their conception of deliberation. Like their liberal counterparts, the antiliberal theorists have not really addressed the fundamental difficulty facing their view. Antiliberals turned to deliberative politics as a way of meeting objections concerning majority tyranny and the other forms of oppression. Antiliberal appeals to shared values, membership, and common purposes need not suggest majoritarianism and oppression if they are supplemented with an account of deliberation which allows for respectful, reasoned disagreement among citizens morally divided. However, it has been shown that the antiliberal accounts of public discourse presuppose that fundamental agreement at deep levels already exists among persons who seem to be divided. Thus, deliberation is not a process by which persons confront real differences and try to cooperatively forge common ground. Regarding the antiliberal view, all differences are merely apparent, and common ground can always be found. In light of social scientific data that suggests deep divisions between persons (R. Putnam 2000), this confidence in underlying commonalities among ostensibly divided citizens amounts to mere wishful thinking. Moreover, it does little to address the liberal worries regarding majoritarianism.[26]

Benjamin Barber's recent book promoting a decidedly deliberativist interpretation of his previously formulated conception of "strong democracy" is entitled *A Place for Us*.[27] The allusion to *West Side Story* (and also to *Romeo and Juliet*) is fitting for reasons probably not intended by Barber. What the play reveals is that, although there is a place for Tony and a place for Maria, there really is no place for Tony *and* Maria. In this instance, art is imitating life: Every communal "place for us" entails a "them" who must occupy some other place. The antiliberal community, the "place for us," seems more a place for like mindedness and sameness, than for difference, cooperation, and tolerance.

Of course, antiliberals will respond that their vision of cooperative community differs from the pathological, intolerant, and oppressive forms of collectivism against which their liberal critics react. In fact, antiliberals often lay the blame for such collectivism at the door of liberalism. Barber writes, "Twentieth century collectivism is in part a consequence of the failure of liberalism to offer a healthy politics of community" (Barber 1998b, 9); and Sandel concurs, "Where political discourse lacks moral resonance, the yearning for a public life of larger meaning finds undesirable expression ... Fundamentalists rush in where liberals fear to tread" (1996, 322; cf. Sandel 1998a, 216–218).

Although they recognize that communities can share and promote a defective moral vision, the antiliberals offer a deliberative theory according to which the aim of public discourse is to align separate wills with the social "we." Deliberation is thus not a mechanism by which the shared moral vision of a given community can be critically evaluated, corrected, or revised. Certain that dichotomies and divisions between "me," "us," and "them" can ultimately be transcended (Barber 1998a, 116–117), the antiliberals propose no deliberative mechanism for dealing with the fundamental disagreements which will inevitably arise in a modern democracy.

In this lies the most serious difficulty with the antiliberal view. As they believe that the material necessary for harmonious, cooperative co-existence lies dormant within citizens, public deliberation is seen by the antiliberals as a prelude to politics, a process by which the latent common political will comes to realize itself in the form of shared purposes, commitments, and ideals. But where there is widespread agreement and a shared moral vision, there is no need for deliberation. Deliberation is a merely instrumental, temporary value to the antiliberal; once a truly political community is achieved through deliberation, deliberative processes may be discarded. This Rousseauian fantasy offers little by way of guidance to citizens who every day confront real disagreement in the public arena. When the promise of a politics of communal "we-ness" fails, as it inevitably will, what shall citizens of modern democracies do?

Whereas the liberals offer a theory of deliberation which restricts vocabularies and agendas to such a degree that there is ultimately nothing left to deliberate *about*, the antiliberals promote a view according to which deliberation, understood as the process of excavating a shared political will, is ultimately unnecessary. Neither style of deliberativism is satisfactory. The liberal conception cannot supply the liberal with the theory of citizenship and participation which his view otherwise lacks. The antiliberal conception does not respond effectively to legitimate worries concerning majority tyranny and community-sanctioned oppression. Furthermore, both types of deliberative theory present a false image of our political situation. The liberals begin from the assumption of irreducible social pluralism and insurmountable difference; they promote a deliberative politics that attempts to ignore such differences so that politics might proceed peacefully despite them. The antiliberals begin from the opposite assumption of a deep but unrealized political community of shared values and common ground; they promote a deliberative politics that places morality at the fore of public discourse. Public discourse is supposed to dissolve differences and transcend disagreement, revealing a shared political will that was there all along.

Just as we cannot determine *a priori* the depth of our disagreements, we cannot begin from the premise that all disagreements are shallow or illusory. Both presumptions represent a dangerous oversimplification of contemporary politics; citizens' interests, values, moral visions, and purposes intersect, overlap, diverge, and conflict in a variety of complex ways. The degree to which citizens are divided at fundamental levels is an empirical matter; it is something which can only be determined in the actual course of citizens coming together to confront each other, neither as sanitized political personae programmed to obey the percepts of reasonable discussion, nor as segments of an immanent communal whole predestined to realize the general will. But rather as persons, with all the attendant complexity, who, for better or worse, share a common political sphere and destiny. What is required, then, is a conception of democratic deliberation and citizenship that can recognize that our political life is characterized neither by irreconcilable difference nor by immanent commonality. There are real conflicts of ideas and purposes that might be ultimately intractable, but are nonetheless legitimately political, and therefore, unavoidable. Likewise, there can be, and sometimes are, real convergences of interests, purposes, and values among persons who may seem hopelessly divided.

In formulating conceptions of deliberation, liberal and antiliberal theorists have put the cart before the horse. Beginning from within a given political framework with antecedent commitments and principles, theorists have conscripted the idea of public deliberation to help repair weaknesses in their general framework of political philosophy. Not surprisingly, we have found that liberal deliberative theories tend to promote or favor decidedly liberal deliberative outcomes, and antiliberal theories do the same with respect to antiliberal outcomes. In neither case is deliberative democracy understood as a political theory in its own right. The deliberative turn in contemporary democratic theory is as yet incomplete. What is needed is a deliberative account of democracy that is not precommitted to liberal or antiliberal goals; we cannot rely upon deliberation to complete an otherwise faulty political program, and we cannot expect deliberativism to resolve the series disputes known as the "liberal-communitarian debate." A viable account of deliberative democracy must be a political theory in its own right.

CHAPTER 6

A Pragmatist Conception of Deliberative Democracy

My objectives thus far have been primarily critical. I have argued that liberal theory is internally conflicted, and consequently, provides insufficient resources to sustain democratic practices under conditions of social pluralism. If we continue to conduct our political thinking within a liberal framework, we should expect increasing nonparticipation, separateness, alienation, intolerance, and distrust among citizens of the sort lamented in much of the current social-scientific literature. I have also argued that antiliberal proposals are insufficient, as well, insofar as they simply react against liberalism; they merely replace the liberal autonomous individual and her fixed preferences with a static community of similarly fixed traditions and a predetermined identity. In both cases, political theory is insufficiently attentive to the existing conditions of political practice. Whereas the dislocated self of the liberals has no motive to participate democratically in politics, the encumbered self of the antiliberals is already so thoroughly ensconced in political relations, that acts of democratic self-government are impossible.

I then turned to recent developments in deliberative democracy. I found that the principal proposals simply reinstated the liberal/antiliberal problem. We may view the debates between liberal and antiliberal deliberativists as a rehearsal of a more fundamental dispute between Kant and Hegel, where liberals are Kantian deliberative formalists, and antiliberals promote a Hegelian deliberative eschatology. Both historically and doctrinally, pragmatism is an attempt to navigate between Kant and Hegel; for this reason, pragmatism may be of use in developing a freestanding deliberative account of democracy. In this chapter, I will lay the groundwork for a pragmatist account of deliberative democracy.

A word must be said about the sense in which the view I shall develop is "pragmatist." I take pragmatism as fundamentally a methodological proposal: Our theories must begin with our practices. However, unlike Rorty and the later Rawls, we do not begin with our practices simply because they are ours. We begin with them because they are practices, and responsible theorizing, especially about political matters, must remain closely tied with what we do. But, again, the "we" in the previous sentence does not entail Rortyan ethnocentrism. According to the pragmatist, we begin with our practices but need not end with them. In fact, the pragmatist maintains that part of the point of philosophizing is to subject to criticism those very practices from which our theorizing begins.

The pragmatist methodological prescription that theory should begin with practice entails a kind of philosophical minimalism. Theory must not only begin with practice, it must remain faithful to practice by keeping in close touch with it. The pragmatist envisions a dynamic theory-practice loop in which each is responsive to the other in an ongoing interaction. Pragmatists are consequently suspicious of high flights of theory; they aspire to keep theory as lean as possible and free from abstract entanglements. As Peirce said, pragmatism seeks to "Dismiss make-believes" (5.416).[1] This, of course, means that the pragmatist recognizes that theory must be incomplete and perpetually subject to revision in light of further practice. Thus, a pragmatist deliberativism cannot be developed fully by a single theorist, and perhaps it cannot be developed *fully* at all; its continuing development is the work of a deliberating democratic polity. Accordingly, the aim of the present chapter is more to raise possibilities and open questions than to present a finished theory.

The pragmatist appeal to practice confronts an immediate problem. Even if it is granted that our theorizing must begin with our practices, there exists the problem of identifying which of our practices we should begin with. It seems that every beginning invites challenge and criticism: Why begin with those practices? Moreover, practices are never simply given, but must always be described and characterized, and any such description or characterization is contestable. Although the pragmatist has given a clear prescription of where to begin, there's still a problem of how to begin. A pragmatist would have it no other way. As we shall see, I take the very practices associated with criticism and contestation as the starting place for deliberative democracy.

The sketch of a pragmatist view of deliberative democracy will proceed in two stages. In the first stage, I shall draw upon some of Cheryl Misak's recent work developing a Peircean justification for deliberative democracy. In full appreciation of the point that theory and practice can never really be separate, the second stage will focus upon democratic practice. I shall argue that the pragmatist focus upon *inquiry* provides resources for a vision of democracy in which justification and practice are fully integrated. I then turn to the issue of social pluralism, and will show that the pragmatist view is sufficiently accommodating of disagreement. Finally, I shall show how my pragmatist view can accommodate some liberal worries. To begin, we must recall a few key points from our earlier discussion of the Guardianship Argument.

Guardianship, Democracy, and Deliberation

I argued in the previous chapter that liberalism was developed as a revolutionary response to arguments supporting the legitimacy of aristocratic and monarchic regimes. Historically, these arguments followed roughly the line of reasoning represented in the Guardianship Argument. The Guardianship Argument draws upon the following two philosophical principles:

> **Political Wisdom Principle.** (1) Normative claims about politics are cognitive, and (2) knowledge of the truth values of normative political claims (i.e., political wisdom) is possible.
> **Epistemarchy Principle.** Political wisdom entitles the politically wise person to a share of political power directly proportionate to his wisdom. Conversely, those lacking political wisdom should lack political power.

Liberals countered the Guardianship Argument with the denial of at least one of these principles. Traditionally, it has been thought that unless at least one of these principles is denied, the Guardianship Argument will succeed, and democracy will have to be abandoned.[2] Democratic politics was, hence, divorced from the epistemological and moral concerns presupposed by Socrates. However, this sundering of democracy from epistemology and political wisdom makes sense only under the kinds of historical circumstances within which liberalism was first proposed but which no longer pertain. Again, where entrenched social homogeneity could be presupposed, as in Locke's England, there was no need for a political theory to address questions of citizenship and the public good. Under current conditions of social pluralism and disagreements at fundamental levels, however, a politics which ignores substantive questions of the sort that Socrates insisted upon pressing will, as Sandel has argued "generate its own disenchantment" (1996, 24) in the form of the dwindling participation, eroding civility, and dissolving trust which is now evident. Yet, as the *Republic* shows, a politics expressly aimed at truth and wisdom will be hostile to democracy. Hence, the challenge of a post-liberal democratic theory is to "let truth be the guide without illegitimately privileging the opinions of any putative experts" (Estlund 1997, 183).

It is important to note that the Guardianship Argument was originally framed within the context of an entire metaphysical and epistemological system that we shall call "Platonism." Although few today explicitly accept Platonism as a viable philosophical position, many who attempt to respond to the Guardianship Argument tacitly, or perhaps unwittingly, accept the epistemological notions characteristic of Platonism. In this way, democratic theorists have conceded a crucial element of Socrates' case against democracy. This is a mistake. As Plato himself showed in the *Parmenides*, the epistemological and metaphysical assumptions of Platonism are untenable. They must be rejected if a viable case for democracy is to be made.

According to a standard reading of Plato, Socrates understood the politically wise person, the philosopher king, to be one who has knowledge of The Form of the Good. On the basis of this knowledge, the politically wise person could design public policy to realize particular goods in the political realm (500c–e). Although the politically wise person approaches knowledge of the Good through dialectic (533b–d), it is actually attained in an act of *theoria*, and intellectual grasping or beholding akin to the way in which one becomes aware of the Sun.[3] As the object of knowledge cannot change (477ff.), the Good is fixed and immutable, and once knowledge of it is attained, it is possessed in its entirety once and for all. Because few people are capable of grasping the Good, and because knowledge of the Good is necessary for legitimate political rule, few persons are fit for political rule. Consequently, the just constitution places political rule in the hands of the few who know the Good.

The feature of this view that is most relevant to our purposes is the idea that the Good is an independent entity, knowledge of which can be grasped in an individual act of apprehension and then applied to action in particular cases. Liberal theorists have tacitly accepted this general epistemological picture even when they have sought to reject the Guardianship Argument. The liberal democrat's typical response that "an adult person is more likely, as a general rule, to understand his or her personal interest better than another person" (Dahl 1989, 70) may obstruct the Guardianship Argument, but leaves in tact the Platonist epistemology of a Good which can be discerned by an individual consciousness. To see this, consider that the traditional democratic response simply replaces talk of external and eternal Platonic entities with talk of internal and fixed individual preferences as the "good" that democratic processes are supposed to track. However, this kind of democratic response is fragile; even if we suppose that there are such things as "interests" and "preferences" in the sense required, the principle that each person is the best judge of his own good (his own interests, or preferences) is not immediately plausible, and tends to degenerate into a vacuous platitude.[4]

The crucial principle underlying Platonism and much of subsequent philosophy is that the cognitivity of moral and political judgments entails a set of metaphysical commitments to moral objects or entities, such as the Good. Once this is supposed, accepting the Political Wisdom and Epistemarchy Principles entails the rejection of democracy. If political wisdom is knowledge of some object, then it is unclear why one should need public discussion to discover it rather than, for example, the research of a few well-trained (political) scientists.[5]

Accepting this Platonist premise, many deliberative theorists have denied that there are political truths which deliberation discovers.[6] According to one prominent strand of deliberativism, which we may call "proceduralist," political deliberation has no epistemic role whatsoever. On proceduralist views, the aim of democratic deliberation is not political wisdom, but the political legitimacy of deliberative outcomes. Open political deliberation generates legitimacy because it guarantees fairness to all at the level of political decision in the form of equal access, reciprocity, and respect.[7]

David Estlund (1997) has identified the trouble with proceduralism. If the proceduralist aims at fairness, then why is deliberation required at all? Surely, there are more economical ways to achieve fairness in political decision. Estlund recommends a coin flip (1997, 176), or a fair lottery among all citizens selecting one to make a given decision (1997, 191) as paradigms of fairness. The intuition that coin flips and citizen lotteries are insufficiently democratic will force proceduralists to articulate a reason to reject these undoubtedly fair procedures, thus leading them to abandon a strictly proceduralist view of deliberative democracy.

Another strand of deliberative theory, which we may call "constructivist," attempts to "define political truth as the outcome of [the] deliberative process" (Sunstein 1993a, 19). Benjamin Barber, for instance, has insisted that "Political truth is made in the context of history and experience," and that "there are no 'true' or 'false' answers, no correct or incorrect positions" with regard to political problems, but only "alternative visions" competing for "communal acceptance" (1984, 169). However, Barber's denial that deliberation is responsive to anything outside itself it tantamount to rejecting the cognitivity of normative political proposals, and therefore, severs an essential connection between deliberative democracy and the Political Wisdom Principle; Barber, hence, invites the kind of objection raised in the preceding chapter. Furthermore, if there are no correct or incorrect political positions, then what is there to deliberate about? If there are no correct and incorrect answers to political policy questions, then deliberation is strictly impossible, and all discourse is merely negotiation or bargaining. Barber's constructivism is no more legitimate than the coin flips rejected by Estlund.

Another position, with which the pragmatist view I favor is closely allied, is committed to an epistemic understanding of deliberation. On an epistemic view, democratic deliberation aims to track the truth, or arrive at correct political policies; the epistemic quality of the results of democratic deliberation generates their legitimacy.[8] There are strong and weak versions of epistemic deliberativism, and the distinction depends upon how strong the commitment to epistemic correctness is. Rousseau is often cited as having held a "strongly epistemic" (Estlund 1993b, 92) theory of legitimacy—a political policy is legitimate, and hence, binding only if it is correct. Weaker versions hold that deliberative outcomes are legitimate even if not always strictly correct; the legitimacy is often said to come from the general reliability of democratic deliberative procedures.

Strong views most clearly invite the antidemocratic implication discussed previously. If the justification for deliberative democracy rests entirely in the epistemic correctness of its decisions, then it is unclear why political power should not be turned over to political experts. The Guradianship Argument looms. Updating Estlund, I call this the "epistemarchy problem." The task of an epistemic deliberativism is to avoid endorsing epistemarchy, while still remaining committed to the general view that the justification for deliberative democracy lies in the epistemic qualities of deliberative processes.

To this end, Estlund offers a view he calls "Epistemic Proceduralism" (1997, 174). Epistemic Proceduralism combines a reliabilist view of democratic deliberation with a Rawlsian insight about the moral requirements a political order must satisfy if it is to remain legitimate. It is this view of moral requirements for political stability that provides his response to the epistemarchy problem. According to Estlund, the problem with epistemarchy is, "Who will know the knowers? No knower is knowable enough to be accepted by all reasonable citizens" (1993b, 71). On Estlund's view, legitimacy requires that no competent citizen be required to forfeit his judgment to an expert. That is, even though the justification for deliberative democracy rests in the epistemic properties of public deliberation, epistemarchy is blocked by normative principles requiring equal participation, fairness, respect, and the like. Estlund writes, "Experts should not be privileged because citizens cannot be expected or assumed (much less encourage or forced) to surrender their moral judgment, at least on important matters . . . " (1997, 183).

A problem with Estlund's view is that it begs the question against epistemarchy, and consequently, fails as a justification of deliberative democracy. The epistemarchist, as we shall call him, is not concerned to satisfy Estlund's requirements for legitimacy. The epistemarchist is not moved by Estlund's consideration that no philosopher king will be able to win the consent of large populations; the consent of the foolish and ignorant is, on the epistemarchist's view, of course unnecessary for political legitimacy. For the epistemarchist, the sole requirement for legitimacy is knowledge.

Estlund's response to the epistemarchy problem is weak. What is required is deliberativism that remains appropriately epistemic but which resists epistemarchy in a way that is not question begging. Here is where the pragmatist's minimalism comes into play. By defending a philosophically deflationary theory of truth and deliberation, pragmatism provides the philosophical resources to allow one to accept the Political Wisdom Principle without inviting the antidemocratic entailments. That is, the pragmatist can "let truth be the guide without illegitimately privileging the opinions of any putative experts" (Estlund 1997, 183) because he can follow Bernard Williams' recommendation to "say something" about truth, "but not very much" (Williams 2002, 63). To see this, we shall turn to a pragmatist argument for democracy posed by Cheryl Misak.

Misak's Peircean Justification of Democracy

In her elaboration of a Peircean theory of moral and political deliberation, Cheryl Misak (2000) offers a compelling justification of deliberative democracy. At the heart of her analysis are four related Peircean insights:

1. To believe p is to hold that p is true.[9]
2. To hold that p is true is to hold that p "is a belief that cannot be improved upon, a belief that would forever meet the challenges of reason, argument, and evidence"(Misak 2000, 49).[10]
3. To hold that a belief would forever meet these challenges is to engage in the project of justifying one's belief, what Peirce called "inquiry."
4. One cannot determine on one's own when all the best reasons and evidence have been considered, so the project of squaring one's beliefs with the best available reasons and evidence is an ongoing and essentially social endeavor that requires what Peirce called a "community of inquiry."

In believing that p, one assumes the responsibility of responding to criticisms, meeting challenges, and considering objections. According to the pragmatist, these responsibilities are not simply conventions of conversational politeness, they are, in part, what it is to have a belief. This analysis of belief carries over to assertion. To assert that p is to incur a set of epistemic obligations associated with justifying or defending p against questions, challenges, and countervailing evidence; that is to say, to hold a belief is to be prepared to engage in inquiry concerning that belief. We may summarize these points by saying that to be a believer is to be a truth seeker, to be a truth seeker is to be an inquirer, to be an inquirer is to be a reason giver, and to be a reason giver is to be a reason exchanger, a member of a community of inquirers. Misak writes, "What it is to assert, to make a claim, to believe, to judge is also to be engaged in a process of justification. It is to commit oneself to giving reasons—to be prepared, in the appropriate circumstances, to justify the claim to others, and to oneself" (2000, 94).

The pragmatist thus offers a unified account of belief and truth that is "metaphysically neutral" (Hookway 2000, 77) and that keeps in close touch with human practices of inquiry and discourse (Richardson 2002, 133). In this way, the pragmatist avoids the Platonist implication from the cognitivity of moral and political discourse to an ontology of moral and political facts to which some may be better attuned than others. The pragmatist's deflationism allows her to hold that moral and political discourse is cognitive but resist any specific ontological commitments[11] because cognitivity only requires that assertions be responsive to reason, experience, argument, and the like. In good pragmatist form, Misak contends that "our practice of justifying moral beliefs" and the general "phenomenology of inquiry" lead to cognitivism concerning moral and political claims (2000, 52). The pragmatist also avoids the constructivist position that truth is simply what a given practice produces; on the pragmatist view, truth "goes beyond any particular inquiry" (2000, 57) because inquiry itself must be seen as an ongoing project of confronting beliefs with new arguments and further experience.

The important aspect of Misak's account for our purposes is the justification of deliberative democracy that it entails. According to Misak, the justification of democracy follows directly from what it is to hold a belief, "the requirements of genuine belief show that we must, broadly speaking, be democratic inquirers" (2000, 106). Because believing "involves being prepared to try to justify one's views to others and being prepared to test one's beliefs against the experience of others" (2000, 94), every believer is committed, by virtue of her beliefs, to the enterprise of justification (2000, 74). The enterprise of justification is that of hearing and responding to objections and challenges from all quarters; because to believe is to aim at truth, and to aim at truth is to involve oneself in the enterprise of justification, believing "requires us to listen to others" and to recognize that "anyone might be an expert" (2000, 96). Even the critic of democracy, insofar as she holds beliefs at all, "is committed to having her beliefs governed by reasons" so such a critic "is committed, whether [she] acknowledges it or not, to debate and deliberation" (2000, 106). The commitment to debate and deliberation is a commitment to the basic features of democracy: Deliberators are equal participants in the discussion, with equal access to the conversation, whose voices must be listened to and whose considerations must be addressed.

By way of contrast, let us consider a view that is similar to Misak's proposed by Amy Gutmann and Dennis Thompson. According to Gutmann and Thompson,

> Citizens who owe one another justifications for the laws that they seek to impose must take seriously the reasons their opponents give. Taking seriously the reasons one's opponents give means that, at least for a certain range of views that one opposes, one must acknowledge the possibility that an opposing view may be shown to be correct in the future. This acknowledgement has implications not only for the way they regard their own views. It imposes an obligation to continue to test their own views, seeking forums in which the views can be challenged, and keeping open the possibility of their revision or even rejection. (2000, 172)

Elsewhere, they write,

> The process of mutual reason-giving further implies that each participant involved take seriously new evidence and arguments, new interpretations of old evidence and arguments, including moral reasons offered by those who oppose their decisions, and reasons they may have rejected in the past. "Taking seriously" means not only cultivating personal dispositions (such as open-mindedness and mutual respect) but also promoting institutional changes . . . that encourage reconsideration of laws and their justifications. (2003, 43)

As we noted previously, Gutmann and Thompson offer an account of why citizens "owe one another justifications" and must "take seriously" each others' views that is based in a prior commitment to characteristically liberal values such as reciprocity, publicity, and accountability (2000, 167–170), which are, in their view, "partly independent" of the deliberative process itself (1996, 366, n. 18). Accordingly, Gutman and Thompson's view is importantly different from Misak's. The pragmatic justification for deliberative democracy does not rely upon prior moral agreement upon a set of liberal values, but begins with the practice of seeking justifications for political and moral claims; the claim is that this very process commits one to many of the deliberativist's principles. Misak thus avoids begging the justificatory question in favor of the liberal democrat.

Misak's argument, hence, bears some resemblance to the discourse-theoretic arguments for democracy advanced by Habermas (1990; 1996). On Habermas's view, democracy is a necessary *presupposition* of all proper communication, for communication *itself* requires that "participants coordinate their plans of action consensually, with the agreement being reached at any point being evaluated in terms of the intersubjective recognition of validity claims" (1990, 58). That is, proper communication is necessarily nonstrategic and aimed at reasoned consensus among equal discursive participants rather than mere persuasion and manipulation. This entails that radically antidemocratic speech involves a *performative contradiction*; the very act of expressing a radically antidemocratic position is inconsistent with the very conditions under which such speech acts are possible.

Misak is correct to emphasize a crucial difference between her view and the discourse theory of Habermas. In response to Habermas's transcendental argument and his view of the "inescapable presuppositions" of discourse (Habermas 1990, 89), Misak replies, "It seems that people do communicate—do speak and utter statements to others—without presupposing the things that Habermas . . . [insists] are undeniable" (2000, 41). Misak's pragmatism is far less ambitious. Instead of seeking for a transcendental proof of the legitimacy of democracy, Misak remains a naturalist[12] by appealing only to practices of belief and assertion. As such, her justification of democracy cannot muster the tone of metaphysical necessity that often accompanies the Habermassian view, but it is precisely because her account is not mired in issues concerning the adequacy of transcendental arguments and the other difficulties that Habermas's arguments invite, that her account seems less stipulative and is thus less controversial.[13]

But the modesty of Misak's pragmatic justification comes at a price. What can Misak say to the antidemocrat who denies that he is a truth seeker? One could easily imagine an opponent of democracy, such as the *Republic*'s Thrasymachus, arguing that his beliefs aim not at truth but at power and domination. Misak correctly points out that the pragmatist "is not committed to a 'we must talk with everyone all the time' attitude" (2000, 148); there are some persons in some contexts with whom the pragmatist might reasonably refuse to engage. The point is that we must take these matters on a case-by-case basis; the pragmatic deliberativist attempts to find some level at which the radical antidemocrat properly asserts a belief and engages there.[14] The pragmatist expectation is that there will be some point at which even the most radical antidemocrat will commit to the truth of his beliefs, and consequently, involve himself in the process of reason giving and argument. Hence, although the pragmatist cannot claim with Habermas to have produced an unassailable proof of democracy, one that can refute all antidemocratic challenges; she need not resign herself to the question-begging liberal presumptions of Gutmann and Thompson, she can do better than the "conversational restraints" of Rawlsian public reason, and she can offer a more compelling vision than the Rortyan ironist.

Aims of Deliberative Democratic Practice

Misak's justification of deliberative democratic political arrangements follows from Peircean insights concerning the internal connections among belief, truth, and inquiry. But truth seeking ensures neither truth acquisition nor consensus, so inquirers must engage in the ongoing project of justification by continually subjecting their beliefs to the test of further experience and argument. Hence, the practice of inquiry involves not only the aim of truth, but also the secondary goal of maintaining and extending the material and social conditions under which inquiry can continue. Whereas the primary aim provides the justification for deliberative democracy, the secondary aim provides the basis for a pragmatic conception of democratic practice.

Pragmatists often articulate their vision of democratic practice by means of an analogy with the practice of scientific inquiry. Although this aspect of pragmatism is sometimes misunderstood as a quasi-positivist insistence that all real questions are scientific questions, the pragmatist sees science not as some privileged tribunal, but as an especially well-refined instance of those intellectual processes we engage in when confronted with a problem of any sort. The pragmatist sees science "not as privileged, but as distinguished epistemically" (Haack 1998, 94). There are a few general features of scientific inquiry that are useful in developing a view of democratic practice. Just as scientific inquiry is a cooperative effort directed primarily toward the resolution of specific problems, deliberative democratic citizens are to reason together with the objective of arriving at workable solutions to political problems. Just as the products of scientific inquiry are experimental hypotheses and thus are subject to continual test and revision, the products of citizen deliberations are hypotheses to be tested and evaluated against the problems to which they are supposed to respond. As scientific inquiry is an ongoing endeavor of verifying and confirming scientific theories and proposals, the deliberative process is likewise ongoing; continued deliberation is necessary for purposes of confronting new problems, revising old conceptions when circumstances require, and correcting the products of prior deliberation. Lastly, scientific inquiry accumulates results in the form of theories and claims that, although never proven, are relatively well-confirmed and may be presumed in current inquiries. Similarly, deliberating citizens confront problems armed with the results, conceptions, and principles that have emerged from previous deliberations. That is, present deliberations presume and employ what may be called a "background theory" of well-entrenched political principles. Political justification does not begin from scratch with every occasion for deliberation; some principles, procedures, and facts must be assumed at the start.[15]

By way of summary, we may say that the pragmatist sees political deliberation as a continuing enterprise focused on experimentally responding to problems within a context in which both previous deliberative outcomes and new considerations are operative. Although this view of political deliberation draws heavily from scientific practice, we ought not take the analogy too strictly. Whereas the ultimate aim of political deliberation is truth, the practical pressures of politics often require that decisions be made and actions be taken prior to the time at which inquiry can be fully engaged. Many political actions must be made on the basis of limited applications of inquiry. Hence, the epistemic character of democratic deliberation derives from its epistemic reliability over time rather than at each deliberative outcome; democratic deliberation, understood as an ongoing enterprise, is "the most effective political means currently available to solve complex social problems" (Dryzek 2000, 173). Given the dynamic nature of political phenomena and the pressures of political decision, what is required for generating wise solutions to political problems is a continual feedback mechanism by which citizens can respond to, react to, and work through a shared and complex political world. Public deliberation is this feedback mechanism. It is properly engaged when it addresses political problems in a way that not only resolves the problem, but extends the conditions under which inquiry can commence in the future (Bohman 1996, 240).

Mechanisms of public inquiry require institutional support. A deliberative politics will draw upon many of the institutions associated with liberalism. These include a constitution under which citizens are entitled to equal treatment and equal access to the political process; a system of political representation under which citizens elect representatives who are accountable to their constituents; a legal system that provides guarantees of freedom of speech, assembly, and association; a free press and open access to diverse sources of information; a public system of education; and a guarantee of some degree of economic and material security (Knight and Johnson 1997). However, we note that the justification for these arrangements lies not within a comprehensive doctrine of natural rights or some deep theory of human nature; they are seen rather as especially well-confirmed political hypotheses. They maintain the conditions under which deliberation functions best, and hence, are means to the maintenance, realization, and further development of democracy. Hence, Sunstein, "Liberal rights are pervasively democratic. One of their prime functions is to furnish the preconditions for democratic deliberation" (1993a, 248). We add that the precise nature of these rights—issues regarding their application and extent, and disputes concerning how conflicts among them should be resolved—cannot be set in advance by political theorists, but rather are *themselves* questions for public deliberation.

Citizenship and Virtue

Properly deliberative institutions may yet fail to realize the ideal of deliberative democracy if citizens do not or cannot properly deliberate. Misak's analysis has shown that genuine believers (2000, 106) and proper asserters (2000, 65) must be deliberative democratic inquirers; however, as Haack has emphasized, there are several species of "pseudo-inquiry" (1998, 8), and several species of improper or corrupt belief. Peirce emphasized this in his essay on "The Fixation of Belief" (1877). Peirce observed that people often believe on the basis of insufficient reasons, or on the basis of supposed reasons that are not reasons at all; moreover, Peirce noted that when confronted with the inadequacy of the grounds of their beliefs, people often remain tenacious and refuse to revise their beliefs. Where citizens cannot properly engage in the project of justification, there can be no deliberative democracy; thus it is essential to a pragmatic deliberativism to further specify what public deliberation is and what it requires of citizens.

Public deliberation is not simply conversation. Persons getting together and talking about politics will in itself accomplish little. In fact, if one turns to the current arenas of public discourse, such as talk radio, afternoon confessional television, evening debate programs, and internet newsgroups and discussion lists, one is likely to be disappointed. In these forums, discussion most often secures little more than the reinforcement of prejudices, a heightened polarity and sense of the intractability of political conflict, and further confirmation that reason and fair mindedness is no match for rhetorical prowess. Judging from these examples, open public discourse facilitates the construction of a Babel rather than a politically wise self-governing community. One may, hence, conclude that the policy of granting greater political influence to public discussion will only strengthen the ability of sophists and demagogues to bewilder the public. Far from a remedy for democracy's discontent, political discourse actually obstructs self-government.[16]

Demagoguery and other forms of discursive manipulation are not the only danger. Cass Sunstein (2003a; 2003b; 2001a, Ch. 3; 2001b, Ch. 1) has called attention to the phenomenon of "group polarization." Group polarization is a well-documented phenomenon that has "been found all over the world and in many diverse tasks"; it means "members of a deliberating group predictably move toward a more extreme point in the direction indicated by the members' predeliberation tendencies" (2003a, 81–82). Importantly, the polarization is even more pronounced in groups that "engage in repeated discussions" over time (2003a, 86). Hence regular political discussion among like-minded persons "should produce a situation in which individuals hold positions more extreme than those of any individual member before the series of deliberations began" (2003a, 86). Even in the absence of the manipulation, skilled rhetoricians and "spin doctors," discussions among well-intentioned and sincere persons can be corrupted. Sunstein argues that the best protection against group polarization is to ensure that political deliberation always includes dissenting voices and concerns. This means that political deliberators must actively expose themselves to increasingly wider "argument pools" (2003a, 93). This, in turn, means that public deliberation, when properly conducted, will be fraught with conflict, controversy, and dissent (Sunstein 2003b). Thus, the image promoted by some theorists of a deliberative politics that avoids conflict and cultivates peaceful consensus—whether through artificial "conversational restraints" or homogenizing appeals to "we-ness" and a "common good"—is chimerical.[17]

Dealing with these realities of the social dynamics of public discourse, Sunstein has argued that discursive manipulation and group polarization are minimized when deliberators are regularly exposed to "arguments to which they are not antecedently inclined" (2003b, 164). Sunstein, hence, calls for a "new deal for free speech" (1993a, 23) and series of media and communications initiatives designed to widen the "argument pools" (2003b, 164) that citizens encounter. To cite one example, he recommends legislation requiring websites of political organizations—especially those expressing politically extreme viewpoints—to include links to sites that express contrary perspectives (2001a, 182ff.).

However, Sunstein recognizes that legal interventions of the sort he proposes are by themselves not sufficient. A system of free speech cannot do what it is supposed to do unless citizens are motivated to seek out deliberative engagement with perceived political opponents. That is, a "well-functioning democracy" must cultivate a "culture of free speech" and "not simply the legal protection of free speech" (2003b, 110). Describing a culture of free speech, Sunstein writes,

> It encourages independence of mind. It imparts a willingness to challenge prevailing opinion through both words and deeds. Equally important, it encourages a certain set of attitudes in listeners, one that gives a respectful hearing to those who do not embrace the conventional wisdom. (2003b, 110)

The attitudes Sunstein identifies are not merely adjuncts to or byproducts of his conception of deliberative democracy, they are *essential* to it. In the absence of such attitudes, Sunstein's proposed legislation will be seen as no more than an unjustified interference with individual liberty and free expression, and may consequently give further impetus to the insular tendencies they are intended to combat.

Following Sunstein, we are lead to the view that proper deliberation requires deliberators who embody certain intellectual traits or epistemic virtues.[18] The view I am offering takes an Aristotelian and civic republican tack in promoting a virtue-based account of democratic discourse.[19] Unlike other deliberativists, I derive my understanding of deliberation neither from a transcendental deduction of an "ideal speech situation" from "inescapable presuppositions" of communication, nor from the substantive political program I favor; rather, I turn to instances of deliberation and attempts to extract from these the general characteristics of proper deliberation. Of course, this process is itself experimental and fallible, always open to challenge.

One of the striking features of our current modes of political discourse is how attuned they are to questions of epistemic character. Politicians frequently rebuke their opponents for being insincere, hypocritical, driven by ideology, unresponsive to criticism, and beholden to judgment impairing outside interests. Best-selling books of political commentary promise to offer a "no spin zone" (O'Reilly 2003) of "fair and balanced" analysis; they aim to admonish "liars" and "cons" (Franken 2003; Corn 2003; Coulter 2003; Palast 2003), to dismantle the "propaganda machine" (Conason 2003), and expose "bias" in the news media (Alterman 2003; Goldberg 2003). Popular television and radio political programming is similarly driven by a rhetoric of truthfulness, epistemic integrity, and intellectual courage. In this way, contemporary political discourse upholds an image of proper public deliberation according to which responsible discussion is informed, balanced, responsive to reasons, open, and inclusive. Of course, this is not to say that current discourse exemplifies this image; charges of bias and dishonesty, such as claims to integrity and truthfulness, are most often rhetorical tools for smearing opponents. But the fact that the rhetoric is so popular suggests that it is effective, and the fact that it is effective speaks to the degree to which the implicit image of proper deliberation is generally endorsed.

This implicit image of proper deliberation complements the general account of the aims of deliberation previously offered. Recall that political deliberation can be characterized in terms of two related aims. Primarily, political deliberation, like all deliberation, aims at truth. However, given the pressures of practical decision and the nature of truth seeking, political deliberation locally aims to address political problems in ways that avoid further problems and that maintain, and, if possible, expand the conditions under which deliberation may continue. Pursuit of these aims requires that deliberators embody roughly the kinds of epistemic traits implicitly advocated in the popular arena. Hence, drawing upon the popular image, we may identify dispositions and attitudes that constitute what may be thought of as "deliberative virtues." When deliberators embody these virtues, their deliberations are more likely to generate politically wise results. The following list is not exhaustive, but preliminary; likewise, the descriptions following each virtue are suggestive rather than definitional.

The Virtues of Deliberation: A Preliminary List

Honesty. Honesty in deliberation is the disposition to follow evidence and weigh various factors relevant to a problem, and a willingness to base decisions upon such considerations. The honest deliberator enters into the deliberative process with the recognition that his own favored ideas and conceptions might, upon examination, turn out to be faulty or parochial and in need of revision or even abandonment; he is open to unpopular or unorthodox proposals. The citizen who is an honest deliberator follows reasons and arguments, not bare interests or preferences. He is fair minded and deliberates "in good faith"; he is, therefore, prepared to change his mind even about very important matters when circumstances require, but he is also prepared to hold firm when necessary.

Modesty. The complexity of political questions is such that it is often impossible to know exactly how a proposed solution will operate once instituted. Sometimes, even well-conducted deliberation will generate solutions which will fail in practice. Even when a proposed solution to a problem is successful, there will be unintended consequences, unforeseen outcomes that constitute new problems. The modest deliberator understands political proposals, not as ultimate resolutions, but as hypotheses to be tried and evaluated in terms of their effects. He seeks workable ameliorations to present problems and is suspicious of panaceas.

Charity. Given the complexity of our world, there exists an understandable and familiar, but nonetheless dangerous, tendency to oversimplify political questions into simplistic categories: "pro" and "con"; "left" and "right"; "conservative" and "liberal"; etc. Such categories are obstructions to deliberation as they aid in the constriction of "straw-men," and hence, block argument and mutual understanding. Excellent deliberators thus embody the virtue of charity; they accept as a default position that their opponents are not simply stupid or misguided or corrupt, but possibly correct. Hence, they are suspicious of polarizations and ideological categories, as well as of easy and obvious solutions to political problems. Accordingly, the charitable deliberator is also willing to listen responsibly to opposing views and to consider them fairly.

Integrity. Self-government through proper collective deliberation is difficult. In addition to these virtues, democratic deliberation requires of citizens the ability to continue working cooperatively on a problem despite set backs, complexity, failures, and adversity; I call this the virtue of integrity. The deliberator who embodies the virtue of integrity understands that, however divided he and his fellow citizens otherwise may be, they nonetheless are joined in the common and continuing undertaking of self-government. He accordingly strives to be fair to his opponents; he tries to place himself in the position of others to better understand their concerns; he seeks not only to refute or disprove opposing views, but to rationally persuade others and, when persuasion fails, strike a reasonable compromise.

Taken together, these character traits foster in the individual epistemically responsible habits of belief, what Misak calls "genuine" belief (2000, 106). The virtuous deliberator is able to recognize relevant considerations, to weigh contradicting considerations, to listen effectively to new considerations, to be critical but open to objections, to articulate her own ideas and suggestions, and to revise her beliefs when reasons suggest that she do so. We may derive a general conception of deliberative virtue from Iris Young's characterization of "reasonableness":

> Reasonable participants in democratic discussion must have an open mind. They cannot come to the discussion of a collective problem with commitments that bind them to the authority of prior norms or unquestionable beliefs. Nor can they assert their own interests above all others' or insist that their initial opinion about what is right or just cannot be subject to revision. To be reasonable is to be willing to change our opinions or preferences because others persuade us that out initial opinions or preferences . . . are incorrect . . . Being open thus also refers to a disposition to listen to others, treat them with respect, make an effort to understand them by asking questions, and not judge them too quickly. (2000, 24–25)

Young's characterization is important because it reclaims the term "reasonableness" from the entrenched later-Rawlsian usage. Recall that on the

Rawlsian picture, a person is reasonable insofar as he holds a reasonable comprehensive doctrine (Rawls 1996, 36). A comprehensive doctrine is reasonable, in turn, insofar as its content is generally compatible with the basic commitments of a liberal democracy (Rawls 1996, 49, n. 1). Hence, on the Rawlsian view, reasonableness is a matter of the *content* of one's doctrine rather than the degree to which one is willing to subject one's view to rational scrutiny. Consequently, even a knockdown argument for an antiliberal doctrine is insufficient to make those who hold it reasonable. By contrast, the view Young has expressed says that reasonableness is a matter of the degree to which one is willing to engage in what I have called the process of justification. Accordingly, to be unreasonable is to be unwilling to exchange reasons.

A view similar to Young's, and fully in line with the view I have been developing, is expressed by Sidney Hook in the form of ten general "ground rules" for democratic argument. They are as follows:

1. Nothing and no one is immune from criticism.
2. Everyone involved in a controversy has an intellectual responsibility to inform himself of the available facts.
3. Criticism should be directed first to policies, and against persons only when they are responsible for policies, and against their motives or purposes only when there exists some independent evidence of their character.
4. Because certain words are legally permissible, they are not therefore morally permissible.
5. *Before* impugning an opponent's motives, even when they legitimately may be impugned, answer his arguments.
6. Do not treat an opponent of a policy as if he were, therefore, a personal enemy of the country or a concealed enemy of democracy.
7. Because a good cause may be defended by bad arguments, after answering the bad arguments for another's position, present positive evidence for your own.
8. Do not hesitate to admit lack of knowledge or to suspend judgment if evidence is not decisive either way.
9. Only in pure logic and mathematics, not in human affairs, can one demonstrate that something is strictly impossible. Because something is logically possible, it is not therefore probable. "It is not impossible" is a preface to an irrelevant statement about human affairs. The question is always one of the balance of probabilities. And the evidence for probabilities must include more than abstract possibilities.

10. The cardinal sin, when we are looking for truth of fact or wisdom of policy, is refusal to discuss, or action which blocks discussion.[20] (2002, 294–295)

When citizens conduct their arguments according to these prescriptions and embody these dispositions, when they are reasonable, collective deliberation is best able to achieve the aims of deliberation, and hence, to achieve epistemically wise outcomes. A civil society of reasonable citizens is necessary to the development of a proper democracy, a "republic of reasons" (Sunstein 1993b, 17).[21] Of course, virtuous deliberation does not guarantee that mistakes will never be made. It is important to note, however, that no process of political decision—democratic or otherwise—will be infallible. The principal strength of the deliberative account I am proposing is that it is able to incorporate the fact of human fallibility into democratic politics. Insofar as it treats political proposals as hypotheses for responding to political problems and thus requires continuing deliberation, a pragmatist deliberative democracy is self-correcting and open ended. Moreover, insofar as it avoids both liberal proceduralism and antiliberal constructivism, the pragmatist view can countenance critical reflection not only upon its outcomes but also on its own processes; in this way, pragmatic deliberation is self-reflexive and can meet Bohman's call for "more public deliberation about the nature of democracy" (1996, 21).

The reflexive character of proper deliberation is not limited to concerns regarding deliberative processes and institutions. Due in part to what Jon Elster has called "the civilizing force of hypocrisy" (1998, 12), and what David Miller has characterized as the "moralizing effect of public discourse" (2003, 190), engagement in public discourse cultivates the virtues of deliberation and hence makes for better citizens (Mansbridge 1999). When citizens are called upon to engage with each other in the project of justification, they come not only to see their opponents' views in a different, more civil light, but also to see their own views differently. Virtuous deliberators recognize that their beliefs must be subjected to close scrutiny and tough criticism; they, hence, seek out new and more challenging interlocutors and remain open the possibility of refutation and revision.

I have now laid out the basics of a pragmatic account of deliberative democracy. I have drawn Misak's work to show that pragmatist insights concerning the internal connections among belief, truth, and inquiry provide a compelling justification for deliberative democratic political arrangements. Building upon this strategy, I then argued for a pragmatic conception of deliberative democratic practice according to which deliberation is best understood in terms of a set of intellectual dispositions or virtues. I now turn to address two topics central to the earlier chapters of this study: social pluralism and liberalism.

Pragmatic Deliberativism and Social Pluralism

My appeal to deliberative virtues will raise objections of the sort liberal theorists bring against civic republicans. It will be said that any vision of democratic politics that makes central any sort of virtue will inevitably involve the suppression of difference, the quashing of individuality, and the general homogenization of society under a common substantive moral image. In other words, it will be objected that the deliberativism I have proposed is insufficiently pluralistic.

There exists a sense in which this objection is correct: If accommodating social pluralism means that no particular values shall be implicated in political theory, then the pragmatist view I have sketched is not pluralist. However, note that this version of pluralism renders all political theorizing antipluralist. A plausible appeal to pluralism must admit to some constraints upon the kinds of moral, philosophical, and religious views that a democratic polity must accommodate and accordingly must allow for some appeal to, at the very least, the value of those constraints.

Hence, there is no such thing as a political theory that is purely pluralistic. The question of pluralism is rather the question of how substantive a legitimate political community's moral premises may be. This question may be more helpfully framed in terms of how much *contestation* of values is possible within a given regime. Certainly, the stability of a strictly authoritarian regime relies upon its ability to effectively control, and eventually eradicate, contestation. In fact, we may note that historically, it is the mark of authoritarian regimes to impose a set of answers to "big questions" (Ackerman 1989, 361) by means of what Peirce called the "method of authority" (5.379). Under such regimes, to challenge an official answer to a "big question" is to commit treason, heresy, or, in newspeak, "thought-crime."

However, we must also note that contesting values is a kind of reason exchanging, and so presumes a certain social framework that makes such activity possible. There can be no contestation in a vacuum, for contestation is itself a social act involving, at the very least, the communication to others of one's dissent. Such communication cannot occur without mutual recognition of the values that are being contested and a common understanding of what contestatory activity consists in. That is to say, the sphere of contestation that pluralists seek to protect from the encroachment of political entities such as the state and community can exist only within a certain kind of social order. In the absence of a social order in which certain ideas and values are common renders the contestation of values impossible.[22]

The view I have offered seeks to accommodate concerns for pluralism by identifying a set of epistemic habits which secure the intellectual conditions under which moral contestation is possible and possibly constructive. On the view I am advocating, a democratic regime is best understood as precisely that regime which makes contestation over "big questions" possible, due to the fact that its primary commitments lie not with any "big answers," but rather with the hypothesis that "big questions" must remain "open questions" in need of further inquiry. Accordingly, a democratic regime of the sort I envision must undertake the project of promoting among citizens the intellectual habits requisite to proper inquiry; it must seek to effectively "promote contestability" (Pettit 2003, 152). Of course, a radical pluralist may respond that the very idea that "big questions" should be subjected to further inquiry is itself a "big answer"; therefore, the objection will run, and my pragmatist deliberativism excludes contestation over the values associated with inquiry.

My response to this kind of objection is simple. In order to understand the imagined response from the radical pluralist as an *objection*, I must adopt many of the values associated with inquiry. In particular, I must at the very least acknowledge the epistemic authority of arguments and the cogency of the practice of exchanging reasons. So too, it should be added, must anyone posing an objection to any view. The imagined radical pluralist objection, hence, founders; once extrapolated it renders disagreement impossible (Misak 2004).

There is an additional point worth emphasizing. Although it is certainly the case that the view I advocate presumes the normative validity of a certain set of intellectual habits, it is not the case that those habits are, therefore, placed once and for all beyond question. What is precluded is the contestation of those values *en masse* (Gutmann and Thompson 2000, 172). In given instances, the value of charity, for example, may be challenged, or the extent to which deliberators should persist may be questioned. Challenging and questioning the application of deliberative virtue in particular cases can help clarify and deepen our understanding of reasonableness and help refine our concept of inquiry. However, again, such challenges can exist only within a more general context within which inquiry—in this case, inquiry into inquiry (Dewey 1938)—can commence. A pragmatic deliberativism is compatible with any version of pluralism worth accommodating.

It may be further objected that the epistemic view I have proposed will be agreeable only to those who are prepared to admit that their preferred "big answers" could possibly be incorrect.[23] Yet, a socially pluralistic democracy naturally will be home to persons who are fully convinced of the truth of their answers. Such persons will see no value of entering into a deliberative exchange with those who they see as necessarily mistaken; moreover, as they take themselves to already have the truth, they will see no value in entering into a process of justification or in maintaining conditions under which views can be contested. For similar reasons, those who hold such views will reject the pragmatist analysis of the internal connection between truth and inquiry upon which my deliberativism rests. In short, why should those who contend that they have the truth adopt pragmatic deliberativism?

In response, I again call attention to Cass Sunstein's work on "group polarization" (2001a; 2003a; 2003b). Group polarization shows that John Stuart Mill's (1859) epistemic defense of open critical discussion was correct: Deliberatively confronting those with whom we disagree is essential *even when we have the truth*. For even if our "big answer" is true, if we do not engage opposing views, but instead communicate only with those with whom we agree, our "answer" shall shift progressively to a more extreme view, and thus we lose the truth. Groups of the sort envisioned in the objection under consideration are particularly susceptible to polarization because they are, as the objection states, interested in talking only to themselves. However, this kind of epistemic insularity cannot be defended by an appeal to an interest in the truth, for truth itself is compromised by such insularity. In order to get the truth and hold on to it, we must engage those with whom we disagree. Of course, this view can recognize that, at any given time, there will be a wide variety of conflicting views that nonetheless can be adequately justified by means of compelling reasons. Pragmatic deliberativism does not lament this variety, but sees it as an occasion for further inquiry, and indeed sees such further inquiry as an epistemic necessity. And so again, social pluralism is accommodated.

Deliberativism and Liberalism

I have argued for a conception of deliberative democracy that combines a Peircean-pragmatic epistemology with a civic republican view of democratic politics. According to this view, democratic deliberation aims at wise outcomes and can be achieved only by a community in which citizens embody the requisite epistemic virtues. In the closing chapter, I shall address questions regarding the prospects for cultivating a democratic polity. Having addressed concerns relating to pluralism in the previous section, it remains to show how my deliberativism compares to the liberal approach it is intended to replace.

Liberals will object to my view on the grounds that I have not sufficiently provided for individual protection from the will of the (deliberative) majority.[24] My earlier claim that certain principles and policies—such as the liberal basic rights—are so well established that they may be presumed for purposes of current deliberation in the way that a scientist may presume the truth of general physical laws when conducting his experiments. This will seem flimsy to the liberal. On my account, basic rights to, for example, freedom of expression and assembly are treated as especially useful instruments for maintaining the conditions under which proper deliberation can ensue and continue. As such, they are tentative, and in principle, revisable; should some extreme political circumstances arise, my view might recommend suspension of some basic liberal right. The inability of my view to countenance individual rights in the robust liberal sense will be reason enough for the liberal to reject my deliberativism.

However, should liberals insist on an absolutist theory of individual rights, we must remind them that, if the main critical argument of this study is correct, liberal theory cannot generate a coherent and robust theory of individual rights without jeopardizing its own commitment to social pluralism. The liberal thus cannot have her cake and eat it too; she must either try to get by with a thin, political, not metaphysical account of rights, or surrender her claim to official neutrality. Moreover, we should also impress upon the liberal the fact that we already do accept considerable constraints on basic rights such as freedom of expression. For example, we do not grant constitutional protection to threats, fighting words, bribe offers, and certain kinds of obscenity. That is, the idea of an absolute, unfettered right is a myth. The question the pragmatist view prompts is, on what grounds shall we decide how to interpret and constrain, for example, the right to freedom of expression? On this question, the pragmatist agrees with Sunstein that,

> The American constitutional system is emphatically not designed solely to protect private interests and private rights . . . Instead, a large point of the system is to ensure discussion and debate among people who are genuinely different in the perspectives and position, in the interest of creating a process through which reflection will encourage the emergence of general truths. (1993a, 241)

Basic rights will have to be given a nonabsolutist reading on any view; a pragmatic deliberativism argues that basic rights should be understood as well-established means to the realization of a properly deliberative democratic community. Yes, it is important to emphasize that these means are not externally imposed on the deliberative process, but are internal to deliberation itself. As Dryzek contends, "There are mechanisms endogenous to deliberation that can effectively protect those values that liberals enshrine as rights" (2000, 172). As individual citizens are the primary agents of deliberation, the commitment to deliberation entails that individuals should be guaranteed the means necessary for full participation in public discussion; these will include freedom of speech, assembly, conscience, press, and the like. In spite of liberal worries to the contrary, the pragmatist view can offer sufficient protection for each individual.

I have shown that the deliberativist can offer a plausible response to a fundamental liberal objection: A pragmatic deliberative democracy can extend to individuals the necessary protection from majorities. Recall that one of the difficulties facing liberalism is that of reconciling its emphasis on individual autonomy with a conception of democratic participation and citizenship. A mainstay of the antiliberal critique of liberalism is that liberal individualism can be secured only at the expense of community and the sense of a shared public good that seem requisite for democratic self-government. Antiliberals, hence, promote a politics based upon a social concept of the self, a self that is essentially tied to the community to which it belongs. Liberals charge that the antiliberals' communal political vision of tradition, encumberedness, and shared values are inherently majoritarian and oppressive.

A pragmatic deliberativism can steer clear of both the liberal hyperindividualism that makes community impossible and the antiliberal communitarianism that makes community oppressive; the pragmatist view, hence, can generate a plausible conception of democratic citizenship. The pragmatic deliberativist view does this by emphasizing that citizens are neither encumbered selves helplessly ensconced within fixed historical or moral traditions and communities, nor atomic and autonomous agents of ex nihilo self-creation. We rather are, for better or worse, sharers in a common social-political world and the joint inheritors of political institutions, historical traditions, ideas, principles, conflicts, and problems. This social-political world is dynamic and fluctuating, it requires that we respond to it —indifference, nonparticipation, and self-absorption are responses. The pragmatist maintains with the antiliberals that democratic self-government requires a sense of community and shared purpose among citizens; it accordingly rejects the liberal aspiration to a neutral politics and accepts the antiliberal claim that the state must play a formative role in the lives of citizens. Yet the pragmatist also affirms, with the liberals, the need for individual protections against majority tyranny and oppression.

One can endorse a formative state and resist community tyranny. To do this, one denies that the kind of community requisite to self-government must be a community of shared moral commitment. In contrast with the antiliberals, I contend that the state's formative role is that of developing in citizens the intellectual habits necessary to proper deliberation rather than that of imposing a common moral vision. A democratic community is realized by citizens who, no matter how divided they may be at the level of philosophical, moral, and theological essentials, are nevertheless committed to a common method of addressing the political problems which they jointly confront. Seyla Benhabib has framed this point well,

> We cannot resolve conflicts among value systems and visions of the good by re-establishing a strong unified moral and religious code without forsaking fundamental liberties. Agreements in societies living with value-pluralism are to be sought for not at the level of substantive beliefs but at that of procedures, processes, and practices for attaining and revising beliefs. (1996b, 73)

James Bohman argues similarly, "What is reasonable is not the shared content of political values, but the mutual recognition of the deliberative liberties of others, the requirements of dialogue and the openness of one's own beliefs to revision" (1996, 86).

In this way, the democratic state's formative role is epistemological, and not moral. Through public civic education and other public institutions, the democratic state must endeavor to develop in citizens the capacities and dispositions characteristic of excellent deliberation. As proper deliberation generally requires that individuals, the primary agents of deliberation, be protected in various ways, the deliberativist may endorse a roughly liberal set of basic rights; deliberators must be free to express themselves, they must be free to assemble in public and address their fellow citizens, they must be able to access information and news provided by a free press, and so forth. Unlike the liberals, who are unsure of why they are committed to these basic principles, the deliberativism I am promoting, grounds basic rights in the processes of democratic deliberation; individual rights are instruments to political wisdom, tools for crafting a "republic of reasons," not endowments or possessions granted from unknown or other worldly sources. Firmly grounded in the praxis of democratic deliberation, individual protections are rendered more secure and less susceptible to misinterpretation than in the liberal view (Dryzek 2000, 172).

CHAPTER 7
Toward a Deliberative Culture

Contemporary books on democratic theory frequently close with a series of more or less explicit policy and institutional recommendations. Books offering deliberative models of democracy are no exception.[1] However, no consistent deliberativist can provide such recommendations because the fundamental claim of the deliberative democrat is that questions of political policy must be decided by means of public deliberation. Nonetheless, as I have developed a deliberativism that relies upon a view of the epistemic traits necessary for proper citizenship, and furthermore, calls for democratic states to actively promote those traits among its citizens, I must admit that proper democracy can be cultivated only under certain social and political conditions. Recalling Sunstein's point that deliberative democracy is not simply a matter of law, but of culture (2003b, 110), no deliberativist can avoid discussion of the social conditions that must prevail before a deliberative politics can be realized.

Thus, the deliberative theorist appears to be caught in a difficult bind. Any comprehensive discussion of social policy risks contradicting the very essence of deliberative democracy, whereas a theory that leaves questions of policy open runs the risk of seeming purely theoretical and perhaps naïve. A successful navigation through this difficulty requires the identification of those social features that are already in place which, if properly developed, could further realize a deliberative democracy. Put another way, the cultural conditions necessary for a deliberative democracy cannot be simply presumed in fully developed form or imposed from above by democratic theorists, but must be forged from existing cultural conditions. In this brief concluding chapter, I consider the prospects for deliberative democracy by examining present cultural factors that can be of use in developing a deliberative culture.

Demandingness and the Local Paradox of Democracy

In the Preface to this study, we confronted the paradox of democracy: Despite the "nonnegotiable" (Shapiro 2003, 1) character of the language of democracy on the stage of international politics, citizens in the world's premiere democracies are growing increasingly more politically ignorant and less politically engaged. Hence, my proposal for a democratic politics based in ongoing critical deliberations among an epistemically virtuous citizenry will raise challenges of the sort associated with the realist and Schumpeterian schools of democratic theory. These challenges have been forcefully articulated most recently by Richard Posner:

> Deliberative democracy . . . is as purely aspirational and unrealistic as rule by Platonic guardians. With half the population having an IQ below 100 . . . with the issues confronting modern government highly complex, with ordinary people having as little interest in complex policy issues as they have aptitude for them, and with the officials whom the people elect buffeted by interest groups and the pressures of competitive elections, it would be unrealistic to expect good ideas and sensible policies to emerge from the intellectual disorder that is democratic politics by a process aptly termed deliberative. (2003, 107)

Here Posner runs together a general skepticism for any deliberative proposal with two more specific objections. First, he claims that citizens lack the *interest* in political questions necessary for deliberative politics; second, he claims they lack the *aptitude* for deliberation regarding complex political questions. Although Posner's skepticism is understandable, his objections are not decisive. I shall take up the *aptitude* concern first, and then address Posner's claim regarding citizens' *interest* in democratic politics.

The model I have proposed is not immediately susceptible to Posner's aptitude concern because it does not countenance a direct democracy of omniscient citizen statesmen who constantly deliberate about complex and pressing issues confronting the modern nation state. Rather, the view I have proposed is decentralized in that it does not see the state as the only or primary locus of democratic activity. That is, similar to other deliberativists, I countenance levels or spheres of democratic association. At the highest levels of national politics, citizen participation in policy making must be mediated by representative bodies of various sorts, and of these bodies, some will be official (such as congressional representation) and others unofficial (such as citizen advocacy institutions, watchdog groups, and grass roots movements). In certain cases, the views of experts and specialists will carry special weight. But as associations become more local, participation should become more direct, and decision should be more fully in the hands of those affected. There is, therefore, what we might think of as a "division of labor" (Bohman 1999) among different spheres of democratic association. However, this division must not be understood as a discontinuity among the different political spheres. The thread that connects the various spheres of democracy is virtuous deliberation.

This reply raises Posner's other concern, namely, that citizens have no interest in engaging in deliberative processes of self-government even at local political levels. In response, we note that contemporary democratic politics and contemporary democratic citizens are deliberative, or at least quasi-deliberative. As mentioned in the previous chapter, popular media of political commentary claim to be engaged in virtuous political reasoning—they claim to be concerned with evidence and truth; they proceed mostly by way of argument and reason exchange; they, at least in speech, uphold the deliberative virtues. Likewise, citizens who participate in the seemingly ever-growing number of call-in and interactive political programs on radio, television and the Internet take themselves to be engaged in what I have called "the project of justification." They cite data, respond to objections, offer criticisms, and present reasons. Most importantly, they emphatically reject the suggestion that their political opinions are merely expressions of perceived interest or raw preference. Of course, it may be the case that despite this deliberative self-image, citizens' political views are driven by simple preferences and the appeals to reasons and objectivity are just a façade. The point is that the deliberative ideal is upheld in all quarters; the fundamentals of a deliberative culture are in place.

Yet facts do not lie, and so we confront the paradox of democracy in its local form: Despite the fact that our current political discourse is driven by a self-image of rationality, inclusivity, and deliberative virtue, "The public's most basic political knowledge is appalling by any normative standard" (Ackerman and Fishkin 2003, 11).[2] What are we to make of the disparity between our political self-image and our political reality?

The lesson Posner draws is that the deliberative character of contemporary discourse is pure pretense. Despite their tendency to present their political opinions as the outcome of sincere assessments of data and evaluations of arguments, citizens in fact "have no interest in debate" (Posner 2004, 42) and care not a whit for reasons and deliberation. Democratic politics is rather to be understood on the model of an economic market founded upon "consumer sovereignty" (2004, 41). Just as consumers see no need for collective discussion regarding "competing brands of toasters," voters are guided not by reasons, but by "their reactions to the presentation of issues and candidates in political campaigns" and by their "experience of living under particular officials and particular policies" (2004, 41). Posner claims that this is the only "realistic" view (2004, 42; 2003, 154).

It is important to note the sense in which Posner takes his view to be realistic. Keeping with his "everyday pragmatism" (2003, 143), Posner employs the term in contrast with 'theoretical' and 'academic'. That is, he intends his view to be essentially descriptive. However, the descriptive character of Posner's view does not mean that it lacks normative force; according to Posner, his view is normatively superior to the deliberative view insofar as it is more accurate (2003, 130) thus "unillusioned" (2003, 145) about politics. But it is not clear that Posner's view is realistic in this sense. Surely, citizens will not recognize themselves in Posner's description; if the modes of popular political discourse previously discussed are any indication, citizens generally understand their own political opinions to be more than simple preferences and so they see their political activities as something different from their consumer activities.[3] To repeat, on Posner's view, these common self-understandings and self-descriptions are in fact misunderstandings and flawed descriptions. Posner has offered a view of the matter that is not simply descriptive but thoroughly theoretical. It contends that people are generally subject to high degrees of self-misunderstanding —perhaps self-deception—about the status of their own beliefs and motives. The model leaves unexplained the mechanism by which this mistake is generated and does not account for the prevalence of the mistake. The local paradox of democracy remains.

Of course these considerations do not constitute a decisive repudiation of Posner's position. However, they do show that Posner has oversimplified the matter by casting his consumer-based model as "realistic" and the deliberative model as "illusioned." Our present choice is not between an unrealistic deliberativist model and a realistic consumer model, but rather between two deeply theoretical accounts. On one of these accounts, citizens are thoroughly confused with regard to the content of their political beliefs and discussions; whereas citizens generally take themselves to be reason responsive, they are, in fact, simply advancing raw preferences. On the other account, we take seriously the epistemic practices and norms implicit in existing political discourse and attempt to devise a view of democracy in which these norms can be more fully engaged and cultivated.

So I am inclined to address the local paradox of democracy from the direction opposite to Posner's. Citizens are sufficiently interested in deliberative engagement, they have the fundamental capacity for such deliberation, and are at least implicitly committed to an epistemically proper conception of deliberation. The prevalence of public nonparticipation and ignorance is due both to a lack of institutional sites of proper deliberation and to a prevalence of forums that promote vicious deliberation.

Current sites of public political discourse are in a fundamental way epistemically akratic. Whereas they profess to uphold the epistemic virtues of honesty, modesty, charity and integrity, they in practice violate them. In the news media, political issues are presented as a competition between prepackaged political platforms by means of market-tested sound-bites; in the name of fair and balanced treatment, political debates in public forums are presented as contests between two specially selected party representatives who simply take turns announcing sloganized versions of their positions. Presentations of national politics are focused almost exclusively upon horse race contests for public office and power, opinion polls, scandal, and exposé (Anderson 1998).[4] Moreover, political reporting is often retrospective rather than prospective; that is to say, it is aimed primarily at recording the actions government has already taken, rather than providing citizens with information about what government must decide in the near future. Accordingly, political decision is presented always as a process out of citizen control. Taken together, these factors undermine deliberation by promoting an image of the political landscape according to which reasoned discussion is ineffectual or, what is worse, meaningless. Lacking proper forums of deliberation, citizens' deliberative capacities are employed in other arenas, hence, our cultural obsessions with conspiracy theories, pseudoscience, and the paranormal. If this is correct, then what we need are more properly deliberative arenas of civic engagement.

The creation and maintenance of such arenas cannot be merely imposed by government though, but must be the outcome of efforts at multiple levels. As noted in the previous chapter, Sunstein (1993a; 2001a; 2003b) has recommended several legislative measures regarding free speech law designed to ensure that citizens are exposed to diverse argument pools and a "heterogeneous public sphere" (2003a, 90). Sunstein's recommendations are worth exploring, but are not by themselves sufficient; as Sunstein himself notes, "the value of deliberation, as a social phenomenon, depends very much on . . . the nature of the process and the nature of the participants" (2003b, 98). As I have said, deliberative democracy is a call for a deliberative political culture. What is required, then, is research into the most effective deliberative processes and the effects of such processes upon citizens' epistemic character; this, in turn, would call for study of large-scale institutions of democratic deliberation.

Reconciling Deliberative Polls and Deliberation Within

James Fishkin's (1999; 1997; 1991) deliberative polling experiments provide a good example of the kind of effort and research that is needed.[5] Fishkin explains the idea of a deliberative poll like this,

> The idea is simple. Take a national random sample of the electorate and transport it from all over the country to a single place. Immerse the sample in the issues, with carefully balanced briefing materials, with intensive, face-to-face discussions in small groups, and with questions to competing experts and politicians developed in those small groups. At the end of several days working through the issues, face to face, poll the participants in detail. (1999, 282)

Deliberative polls are proposed as a way to implement deliberative democracy; they provide "our best glimpse into what a more informed and engaged electorate would be like" (Ackerman and Fishkin 2003, 12). Fishkin writes, "The premise of the deliberative poll is that a small group, a statistical microcosm of the whole, can overcome the rational ignorance of voters in the large-scale nation-state" (1991, 115). As the participants in a deliberative poll have enjoyed the benefits of information and deliberation, the results represent that the electorate "would think if, hypothetically, it could be immersed in intensive deliberative processes"; accordingly deliberative polls are "prescriptive, not predictive," they have a "recommending force" (Fishkin 1991, 81).

Fishkin's model has been criticized by Robert Goodin on the grounds that it is an example of "ersatz deliberation" (2003, 174). According to Goodin, the problem with ersatz deliberation is that, although the initial pool of deliberators may be a representative subset of the entire electorate, there is no mechanism that ensures "the continuing representativeness of the subset" (2003, 175). Goodin explains,

> Naturally, people change their minds over the course of the deliberation (it would hardly be a genuine deliberation at all if they did not, at least sometimes). The question is whether people who started out being representative of the wider community, in all the ways we can measure, are also representative of that wider community in the ways in which they change over the course of the deliberation. (2003, 175)

Goodin's claim is that it "seems unlikely" (2003, 175) that a group that is representative in its predeliberation constitution will also be representative in the way it views change in the course of deliberation. Accordingly, the deliberative poll does not necessarily reflect what the electorate would think if given the opportunity to deliberate. His conclusion is that Fishkin's model is deeply flawed.

As an alternative, Goodin has proposed his own model of deliberative democracy, which he calls "democratic deliberation within" (2000; 2003). Contending that "conversation is useful, but imagination essential" (2003, 228), Goodin criticizes standard deliberative proposals, such as Fishkin's, for being exclusively attentive to the "external-collective" aspects of deliberation and insists that "internal-reflective" modes of deliberation must also be addressed (2003, 179). Goodin calls for citizens to imaginatively "project" themselves into the place of "some specific other" (2003, 181) so that each can "assess what is the right thing to do, from all perspectives" (2003, 228). Goodin acknowledges that such acts of imagination require actual engagement with others, "Nothing fires the imagination, of policy makers or any one else, better than direct engagement with people whom they are trying to call up in their imagination" (2003, 231). His proposal, hence, recommends "site visits" and other activities that will help citizens see for themselves "what life is like in the places and among the people [their] actions will affect" (2003, 231).

The opposition between Goodin's internal-reflective model and Fishkin's external-collective model is overdrawn. Goodin has overlooked some important features of the Fishkin model. Although Fishkin describes his project as aimed primarily at making policy and candidate recommendations that more accurately reflect the true (reflective) will of the people, an important dimension of its democratic potential lay elsewhere. For our purposes, it is not the outcomes of the deliberative polls that are particularly interesting, but rather the effects of the process upon the participants. As Noelle McAfee has noted,

> Participants leave [deliberative events] saying that even when they did not agree with other participants, they did come to see why the others held the views that they did. They came to change their views of others' views. (2004, 54)

In coming to a better understanding of the grounds upon which others hold opposing views, the deliberative participants come to a better understanding of the grounds for their own views and thus gain an enhanced sense of the complexity of the issues. There has yet to be any decisive study of the long-term effects of participation in deliberative polling experiments on future political and civic participation; however, initial studies corroborate McAfee's report that participation in Fishkin style deliberative polls helps cultivate in citizens the kind of civility and deliberative imaginativeness that Goodin emphasizes (Luskin and Fishkin 2002).

Goodin is right that the external-collective models of deliberation are alone inadequate and need to be supplemented by some "internal-reflective" mechanism (2003, 183). Indeed, meaningful face-to-face encounters within large polities are impossible (2003, 228), and so an internal mode of deliberation in which the perspectives of others are made present in imagination is necessary. Yet Goodin's "deliberation within" is admittedly a "preference-respecting model of liberal democracy" (2003, 228), and so not only inherits many of the difficulties involved with preference-based views, but also confronts the difficulties arising from the fact that deliberation often generates shifts in preferences. The internal-reflective properties of deliberation are better understood in terms of the deliberative virtues by which one is able to envision and anticipate others' reasons, concerns, and objections. That is, internal-reflective mechanisms are not simply aimed at recognizing others' perspectives, but at coming to see envisioned others as coparticipants in the project of self-government by engaging reasons and examining beliefs. But again, these activities, when properly engaged, are not merely critical, but also self-critical; the aim is engagement, and honest engagement requires that citizens subject themselves and their own views to scrutiny and critique. I agree with Goodin that democratic deliberation "requires people to make various changes in their behavior, if not their basic character" (2003, 231). However, the view I have presented calls for changes in citizens' epistemic character, and one of the ways in which such changes are effected is by means of involvement in the kind of deliberative engagement encouraged in Fishkin's polling experiments.

Deliberation Day

The view I have proposed thus applauds the spirit of Bruce Ackerman and James Fishkin's call for a grand extension of the deliberative poll by means of a new national holiday called "Deliberation Day" (2003; 2004a; 2004b). Deliberation Day, which would take place "ten days before major national elections" (2004b, 7), would take the form of a national assembly, with citizens spending one day meeting in groups of various sizes to deliberate about and with major political candidates. As with jury duty, Deliberation Day would modestly compensate citizens for their service. Ackerman and Fishkin (2004b) have worked out in depth the logistical and financial details involved in holding such an event, and so I will not canvass this here.

In proposing Deliberation Day, Ackerman and Fishkin aim to combat not only the widespread "civic privatism" (2003, 8) of contemporary democracy but also to "change the nature of the larger political environment" (2003, 12) by affecting the *modus operandi* of politicians and political campaigns. Describing what they see as the "leveraging" potential in Deliberation Day, Ackerman and Fishkin write,

> In plotting their campaign strategies and advertising, politicians and their consultants would use Deliberation Day as a fundamental reference point. They would no longer automatically suppose that candidates were best sold in eight-second soundbites. Throughout the campaign, their eyes would be fixed firmly on the fact that their messages would be subjected to a day-long dissection—and that millions of votes might swing as a result. (2003, 12)

The envisioned shifts in political strategy would generate further shifts in political discourse more generally, and would therefore constitute a major step toward cultivating a deliberative culture. The overriding hope is that Deliberation Day would "come to symbolize a genuine renaissance of civic culture in America" (2003, 25).

In considering a proposal such as Deliberation Day, we again confront skeptical misgivings, and Richard Posner again provides an able critical voice. Claiming that Ackerman and Fishkin "misunderstand what modern political democracy is and should be" (2004, 41), Posner doubts "the value of political debate among ordinary citizens" (2004, 42). He maintains the realistic view that "modern democracy . . . involves a division between rulers and ruled," with the rulers being drawn from "a governing class of ambitious, determined, and charismatic seekers of power" and the ruled voting "candidates for officialdom in and out of office on the basis of their perceived leadership qualities and policy preferences" (2004, 41). Turning to a substantive criticism of Deliberation Day, Posner maintains "widespread deliberation by citizens at large on issues of politics would mainly just reduce the civility of our politics by raising the temperature of public debate, making our politics more ideological, and therefore, more divisive" (2004, 42).

Again, we see Posner claiming to be "merely realistic" (2004, 42) while, in fact, applying a deeply theoretical account of citizen motivation and competence. More importantly, Posner's objection that large-scale deliberation will serve only to reduce civility and increase divisiveness is not born out empirically. Not only does the data from Fishkin's polling experiments suggest that "the very process of engaging in extended dialogue about shared public problems will produce a greater susceptibility to the public interest" (2003, 22), but experiments cited by Sunstein (2003a; 2003b) regarding group polarization show, strikingly, that politics becomes divisive, ideological, and uncivil in the absence of the kind of engagement that

Ackerman and Fishkin aim to induce. Despite his constant appeal to a hard-nosed realism, the substance of Posner's criticism of Deliberation Day is itself driven by Posner's own ideological allegiances and so fails to square with the data.

That Posner's principal objection to Ackerman and Fishkin's proposal is unpersuasive does not undermine his general skepticism with respect to Deliberation Day. Expressing this skepticism with a refreshing frankness, Posner claims, "If spending a day talking about the issues were a worthwhile activity, you wouldn't have to pay voters to do it" (2004, 41). Certainly, Deliberation Day would be a massive undertaking, requiring an enormous investment of time, effort, resources, and money, and there is no guarantee that Deliberation Day would be a success. The Deliberation Day proposal thus involves a significant risk. However, the value of such a national event is not something we can know *a priori*, and it is not something that can be judged according to whether financial incentives would be required to stimulate citizen participation. The worth of Deliberation Day is rather something that can be assessed in terms of its results, both in social-scientific terms and in terms of citizens' experience.

Hence, it is important to keep in mind something that Posner appears to have overlooked. Ackerman and Fishkin are not proposing Deliberation Day as a once-and-for-all panacea for democracy, but rather as an experiment addressed to the amelioration of certain palpable defects in contemporary democracy. Moreover, Ackerman and Fishkin concede that Deliberation Day is surely not the only worthwhile proposal for addressing these defects, and might not be the best possible proposal. Rather, Ackerman and Fishkin see their proposal for Deliberation Day as a single contribution to creative institutional theorizing on the way to a more deliberative culture. Given the amount of effort, planning, institutional support, and financial backing that is currently devoted to conventional national elections, and given the effect such elections are known to have on our political culture, Deliberation Day seems worth a try. Those who find Deliberation Day too cumbersome to be plausible should not conclude, with Posner, that democracy can be only what it presently is; rather, they should develop new, more modest and achievable proposals. There is no reason why there should not be multiple experiments in deliberative politics.

Deliberativism, Activism, and Inclusion

Thus far I have focused on a line of criticism according to which deliberative democracy is an unattainable ideal, a "pipe dream," as Posner would have it (2003, 163). In response, I have pointed to a recent proposal that may help to achieve the kind of deliberative culture that is required by my pragmatist deliberativism. However, not all critics of deliberative democracy focus simply on its plausibility. Some object to deliberative democracy on the grounds that it is an inherently unjust ideal, one that privileges existing power structures and excludes the voices of the oppressed. It remains to consider briefly this line of criticism.

In an essay entitled "Activist Challenges to Deliberative Democracy" (2003), Iris Young aims to "sound a caution about trying to put ideals of deliberative democracy into practice in societies with structural inequalities" (2003, 103). Although Young accepts the fundamental deliberativist idea that "democracy should be conceived and as far as possible institutionalized as a process of discussion, debate, and criticism that aims to solve collective problems" (1997, 400), she contends that this insight must be understood as also involving a "principle of inclusion" (1999, 152) which requires not only that citizens collectively deliberate, but that those deliberations are inclusive of "all interests, opinions, and perspectives present within the polity" (1999, 154).

Any call for greater inclusion in deliberative democratic processes must address questions concerning the extent of the inclusion. The issue is not simply that of the extent to which a democratic polity must actively seek the deliberative input of those committed to morally reprehensible views, though this is, to be sure, an important issue. The call for inclusion also engages questions of the proper response of deliberative democrats to those who reject the deliberative ideal itself. This issue is especially poignant in the case of Young's model because her mechanisms of inclusion are directed toward expanding the democratic conversation by extending access to those who might be otherwise shut out due to their inability to satisfy the norms of deliberation typically presumed by theorists of deliberative democracy. The issue is not that of expanding our conceptions of deliberation so as to include those who want to join the discussion, but cannot; rather, it is that of dealing with those for whom the deliberative ideal itself seems silly, futile, or foolish.

In order to examine this issue, Young stages a dialectical exchange between two imagined characters: A deliberative democrat and a political activist. Noting that they offer opposed substantive ideals of democratic citizenship (2003, 104), Young develops activist responses to two deliberativist criticisms of the activist view of citizenship and then poses four activist challenges to deliberativism. Before turning to these arguments, it will help to review briefly the point of contention among activists and deliberativists as construed by Young.

As Young envisions them, deliberative democrats and political activists share common goals. They both aim to promote justice and to cultivate a more engaged and participatory mode of democratic politics. They diverge on the issue of means. The deliberativist maintains that the most appropriate means for greater justice and more genuine democracy is the cultivation of "sites and processes of deliberation" by which citizens who disagree can publicly engage each other's reasons, arguments, and ideas regarding shared political problems (2003, 104). Deliberative institutions and processes that aim to involve all citizens in public debate are more likely than their aggregative alternatives to "arrive at policy conclusions freely acceptable by all" (2003, 104), and hence, are more apt to promote justice. The deliberative democrat endorses a particular vision of proper democratic citizenship according to which a deliberative citizen should seek by means of reasoned discussion to persuade those with whom she disagrees that their views are mistaken. Accordingly, the deliberativist holds that citizens should seek out those with whom they disagree and rationally engage their arguments in an open forum.

Maintaining that "the normal workings" of our "social, economic, and political institutions" serve to "enact or reproduce deep wrongs," Young's activist sees the "ordinary rules and practices" that govern societal institutions as bound to perpetuate injustice. He[6] concludes that one cannot redress social injustice while working within those rules and practices (2003, 104). Thus, he advocates action designed to disrupt the political status quo. Such action aims to express the activist's outrage and indignation at what he sees as persistent injustice; through such expressive acts, he hopes to call the attention of his fellow citizens to the injustice and to motivate others to act similarly. On the activist view, then, proper democratic citizenship requires direct action in response to injustice. Such action often consists in strategies designed to publicize the injustice, such as picketing, leafleting, and demonstrating (2003, 105); however, when the injustice is severe, citizenship may require obstructive activity such as blocking entrances to buildings, "throwing stink bombs," and similar tactics (2003, 105).[7]

It is easy to anticipate the general line of criticism that each will launch against the other: The deliberativist contends that the activist's call to confrontation is dangerously unreasonable, whereas the activist holds that the deliberativist's exhortations to rational discussion are naïve. Young's activist brings four arguments against the deliberativist; I shall respond to each.[8]

Young contends that the first two activist criticisms can be answered easily, so I shall deal with them quickly. The first two challenges are focused on the failure of existing political institutions and processes to satisfy the ideals of publicity, accountability, and inclusion (2003, 109) that are promoted by the deliberative democrat. First, the activist points to the exclusionary character of existing sites of deliberation, citing the prevalence of structural inequality and power (2003, 108). Second, he criticizes recent measures aimed at inclusion for falling "far short of providing opportunities for real voice, for those less privileged in the social structures" (2003, 112).

Insofar as the activist's criticisms are aimed at the failure of existing institutions to live up to the deliberative ideal, they implicitly accept that ideal. Thus, as Young points out, a deliberativist can agree with the activist that current conditions fall short of the democratic ideal, and can accept the activist's specific criticisms of the existing order (2003, 112). Again, they differ on the issue of means, not ends. The deliberativist holds that processes of continuing public discourse can reveal and remedy the shortcomings of existing institutions and practices whereas the activist doubts that rational discussion can persuade powerful social agents to adopt a more inclusive and democratic mode of politics (2003, 112). Further, the deliberativist may argue that even if the activist's suspicions regarding the efficacy of political deliberation are granted, these suspicions are not in themselves sufficient grounds for rejecting deliberative democracy. Though not ideal, deliberation may still be the best option available for democracy.

Therefore, the activist must formulate a deeper kind of critique, one that calls into question the consistency of deliberativism with its stated goals. The activist raises two further objections that aim to establish that the political program endorsed by the deliberativist actually serves to perpetuate existing obstacles to inclusion and justice.

The activist's first serious challenge focuses upon the economic and social conditions under which even the most inclusive public deliberation occurs. According to the activist, "existing social and economic structures have set unacceptable constraints on the terms of deliberation and its agenda." That is, the activist contends that,

> Going to the table to meet with representatives of those interests typically served by existing institutional relations, to discuss how to deal most justly with issues that presuppose those institutional relations, gives both those institutions and deliberative process too much legitimacy. It co-opts the energy of citizens committed to justice, leaving little time for mobilizing people to bash the institutional constraints and decision-making process from the outside. (2003, 113)

The charge here is that political deliberation, even when conducted according to proper norms of inclusiveness, accountability, and publicity, always takes place within certain institutional contexts that are encumbered by "a given history and sedimentation of unjust structural inequality" that "helps set agenda priorities and constrains the alternatives political actors may consider" (2003, 113). Thus, the deliberativist's exhortation to reasoned discussion amongst those who disagree may, in certain situations, serve to perpetuate the kind of injustice it claims to counteract. Therefore, the objection runs, it is not simply that the deliberative democrat recommends inefficient means to a more just and inclusive democratic politics, she actually endorses a program that implicitly accepts existing institutional arrangements, and hence, perpetuates the most pernicious kinds of exclusion and injustice.

The activist's second challenge alleges not only that deliberation must occur within institutional contexts that are already encumbered by practices of exclusion, but also that discourse itself may be exclusive. That is, the activist maintains that discussion is always conducted within a "system of stories and expert knowledge" that conveys "the widely accepted generalizations about how the society operates" (2003, 116). Explaining further, he contends, "In a society with longstanding and multiple structural inequalities, some such discourses are, in the terms derived from Gramsci, 'hegemonic': Most of the people in the society think about their social relations in their terms, whatever their location in the structural inequalities" (2003, 116). In this way, the very vocabularies in which public discussion is conducted may contribute to the continuation of injustice; that is, discourse itself may be, in a term Young's activist borrows from Habermas (1970), "systematically distorted" (2003, 116). When discourse is systematically distorted, "Parties to deliberation may agree on premises, they may accept a theory of their situation and give reasons for proposals that the others accept, but yet the premises and terms of the account mask the reproduction of power and injustice" (2003, 116).

Young's activist contends that "The theory and practice of deliberative democracy has no tools for raising the possibility that deliberations may be closed and distorted in this way"; in other words, deliberative democrats lack a theory of "ideology" (2003, 116).[9] Thus, the activist "believes it important to continue to challenge these discourses and the deliberative processes that rely on them, and often he must do so by nondiscursive means" such as "pictures, songs, poetic imagery, expressions of mockery and longing performed in rowdy and even playful ways"; such acts are "aimed not at commanding assent but disturbing complacency" (2003, 118).

These two serious activist challenges may be summarized as follows. First, the activist has claimed that political discussion must always take place within the context of existing institutions that, due to structural inequality, grant to certain individuals the power to set discussion agendas and constrain the kinds of options open for consideration prior to any actual encounter with their deliberative opponents. The deliberative process is, in this sense, rigged from the start to favor the status quo and disadvantage the agents of change. Second, the activist has argued that political discussion must always take place by means of antecedent discourses or vocabularies that establish the conceptual boundaries of the deliberation and may themselves be hegemonic or systematically distorting. The deliberative process is subject to the distorting influence of ideology at the most fundamental level, and deliberative democrats do not have the resources by which such distortions can be addressed.

As they aim to establish that the deliberativist's program is inconsistent with her own democratic objectives, this pair of charges is, as Young claims, serious (2003, 118). However, the deliberativism I have proposed is not susceptible to these objections.

The deliberativism I advocate does not engage public political discussion only at the level of state policy, and so does not endorse a program that must accept existing institutional settings and contexts for public discussion. Rather, I have promoted an ideal of democratic politics according to which deliberation occurs at all levels of social association, including households, neighborhoods, local organizations, city boards, and the various institutions of civil society. The long-run aim is to cultivate what I have been calling a deliberative culture, and I have claimed that this task must begin at more local levels and apart from the state and its policies. The deliberativism I adopt promotes a "decentered" (Habermas 1996, 298) view of public deliberation and a "pluralistic" (Benhabib 2002, 138) model of the public sphere; in other words, I envision a "multiple, anonymous, heterogeneous network of many publics and public conversations" (Benhabib 1996, 87). On my view, the deliberativist is, therefore, committed to the creation of "an inclusive deliberative setting in which basic social and economic structures can be examined"; these settings "for the most part must be outside ongoing settings of official policy discussion" (Young 2003, 115).

Although Young characterizes this decentered view of political discourse as requiring that deliberative democrats "withdraw" (2003, 115) from "existing structural circumstances" (2003, 118), it is unclear that this follows. There certainly is no reason why one must choose between engaging arguments within existing deliberative sites and creating new ones that are removed from established institutions. There is no need to accept Young's dichotomy; work must be done within existing structures and within new contexts. As Bohman argues,

> Deliberative politics has no single domain; it includes such diverse activities as formulating and achieving collective goals, making policy decisions and means and ends, resolving conflicts of interest and principle, and solving problems as they emerge in ongoing social life. Public deliberation therefore has to take many forms. (1996, 53)

The second challenge requires a detailed response, so let us begin with a closer look at the proposed argument. The activist has moved quickly from the claim that discourses can be systematically distorting to the claim that all political discourse operative in our current contexts *is* systematically distorting. The conclusion is that properly democratic objectives cannot be pursued by deliberative means. The first thing to note is that, as it stands, the conclusion does not follow from the premises. What is required is the additional premise that the distorting features of discussion cannot be corrected by further discussion. That discussion cannot rehabilitate itself is a crucial principle in the activist's case, but is nowhere argued. Moreover, the activist has given no arguments to support the claim that present modes of discussion are distorting, and has offered no analysis of how one might detect such distortions and discern their nature.[10]

Rather than providing a detailed analysis of the phenomenon of systematic distortion, Young provides (in her own voice) two examples of discourses that she claims are hegemonic. First, she considers discussions of poverty that presume the adequacy of labor market analyses; second, she cites discussions of pollution that presume that modern economies must be based on the burning of fossil fuels. In neither case does she make explicit what constitutes the distortion. At most, her examples show that some debates are framed in ways that render certain types of proposals "out of bounds." But surely this is the case in any discussion, and it is not clear that it is, in itself, always a bad thing or even distorting. Not all discursive exclusions are distortions because the term 'distortion' implies that something is being excluded that should be included. Clearly, then, there are some dialectical exclusions that are entirely appropriate. For example, it is a good thing that current discussions of poverty are often cast in terms that render white supremacist solutions out of bounds; it is also good that pollution discourses tend to exclude fringe-religious appeals to the cleansing power of mass prayer. This is not to say that opponents of market analyses of poverty are on par with white supremacists or that Greens are comparable to fringe-religious fanatics; it is rather to press for a deeper analysis of the discursive hegemony that the activist claims undermines deliberative democracy.

It is not clear that the requested analysis, were it provided, would support the claim that systematic distortions cannot be addressed and remedied within the processes of continuing discourse. There are good reasons to think that continued discussion among persons who are aware of the potentially hegemonic features of discourse can correct the distorting factors that exist and block the generation of new distortions. As Young notes (2003, 116), Bohman (1996, Ch. 3) has proposed a model of deliberation that incorporates concerns about distorted communication and other forms of deliberative inequality within a general theory of deliberative democracy; the recent work of Benhabib (2002) and Goodin (2003, Ch. 9–11) aims for similar goals. The view I have endorsed in this book is capable of addressing these issues as well.

I conclude that, as it stands, the activist's second argument is incomplete, and as such, the force of the difficulty it raises is not yet clear. If the objection is to stick, the activist must first provide a more detailed examination of the hegemonic and distorting properties of discourse; he must then show that prominent modes of discussion operative in our democracy are distorting in important ways and that further discourse cannot remedy these distortions.

My call for a more detailed articulation of the second activist challenge may be met with the radical claim that I have begged the question. It may be said that my analysis of the activist's challenge and my request for a more rigorous argument presumes what the activist denies, namely, that arguments and reasons operate independently of ideology. Here the activist might begin to think that he made a mistake in agreeing to engage in a discussion with a deliberativist—his position throughout the debate been that one should decline to engage in argument with one's opponents! He may say that, of course, activism seems lacking to a deliberativist, for the deliberativist measures the strength of a view according to her own standards. But the activist rejects those standards, claiming that they are appropriate only for seminar rooms and faculty meetings, not for real world politics. Consequently, the activist may say that by agreeing to enter into a discussion with the deliberativist, he had unwittingly abandoned a crucial element of his position. He may conclude that the consistent activist avoids arguing altogether, and communicates only with his comrades. Here the discussion ends.

However, there is a further consideration to raise against the activist. The activist's case against deliberation has presumed that there is but one kind of activist and but one set of policy objectives that activists may endorse. Yet, Young's activist is opposed, not only by deliberative democrats, but also by persons who also call themselves "activists" and who are committed to a set of policy objectives quite different from those endorsed by Young's activist. Once these opponents are introduced into the mix, the stance of Young's activist becomes more evidently problematic, even by his own standards.

To explain: Although Young's discussion associates the activist always with politically progressive causes, such as the abolition of the World Trade Organization (2003, 109), the expansion of healthcare and welfare programs (2003, 113), and certain forms of environmentalism (2003, 117), not all activists are progressive in this sense. Activists on the extreme and racist

Right claim also to be fighting for justice, fairness, and liberation. They contend that existing processes and institutions are ideologically hegemonic and distorting. Accordingly, they reject the deliberative ideal on the same grounds as Young's activist. They advocate a program of political action that operates outside of prevailing structures, disrupting their operations and challenging their legitimacy. They claim that such action aims to enlighten, inform, provoke, and excite persons they see as complacent, naïve, excluded, and ignorant. Of course, these activists vehemently oppose the policies endorsed by Young's activist; they argue that justice requires activism that promotes objectives such as national purity, the disenfranchisement of Jews, racial segregation, and white supremacy. More importantly, they see Young's activist's vocabulary of "inclusion," "structural inequality," "institutionalized power," as fully in line with what they claim is a hegemonic ideology that currently dominates and systematically distorts our political discourses.[11]

The point here is not to imply that Young's activist is no better than the racist activist. The point rather is that Young's activist's arguments are, in fact, adopted by activists of different stripes and put in the service of a wide range of policy objectives, each claiming to be just, liberatory, and properly inclusive. In light of this, there is a question the activist must confront. How should he deal with those who share his views about the proper means for bringing about a more just society, but promote a set of ends that he opposes?

It seems that Young's activist has no way to deal with opposing activist programs except to fight them or, if fighting is strategically unsound or otherwise problematic, to accept a Hobbesian truce. This might not seem an unacceptable response in the case of racists; however, the question can be raised in the case of any less extreme, but nonetheless, opposed activist program, including different styles of politically progressive activism. Thus it seems that an activist cannot avoid endorsing a politics based upon interest-based power struggles amongst adversarial factions.

The deliberativist advances several criticisms of "adversary democracy"; most important among these for present purposes is the criticism that adversarial modes of democratic politics tend to discourage participation, increase exclusion, occlude options, squelch voices, and cultivate "civic privatism" (Ackerman and Fishkin 2003, 8). Early in the discussion, the activist claimed to share the deliberativist's goal of cultivating a more participatory, communicative, inclusive, and engaged democratic politics. However, if the preceding argument is sound, the activist's mode of political engagement is in practice inconsistent with these goals; more importantly, a deliberative democracy of the sort I have proposed is fully capable of—perhaps even essential to—realizing them.

Conclusion

In this book, I have argued that liberalism cannot provide sufficiently firm ground for democratic politics because it cannot produce a compelling account of democratic citizenship. I have proposed a vision of deliberative democracy that is civic republican insofar as it recognizes that the state must engage in the formative project of cultivating the character traits requisite for democratic citizenship. But what are the requisite character traits? Employing some Peircean-pragmatist insights concerning the nature of justification and inquiry, I developed a view of deliberative democracy that locates the essentially civic virtues within the processes of epistemically proper deliberation. Hence, I sketched an account of the *deliberative virtues*, traits of epistemic character that enable citizens to deliberate well about collective political problems. These virtues and the project of cultivating them, I contend, are robust enough to sustain a meaningful democratic citizenship, but thin enough to eschew well-placed liberal concerns of intolerance, oppression, and community tyranny.

As my discussion of some of the prospects for a deliberative culture suggests, the formative project of cultivating proper epistemic habits implicates no substantive vision of the good life, and therefore does not threaten moral diversity or individual moral autonomy. Of course, the deliberative virtues are not neutral in the liberal sense; some values are implicated in any political proposal. The deliberative model I have proposed commits to a moral vision that is minimal, requiring the recognition of only those values requisite to deliberation itself. It envisions a deliberative public that, despite deep disagreements among individual citizens, is perpetually engaged in the joint project of self-government at multiple levels of social association. That we are the joint inheritors of a common political world cannot be denied; neither can it be doubted that our current practices and attitudes shape our political future. This is a future that will also be shared. Whether it will be shared in the way that participants in a common undertaking share the rewards and responsibilities of the cooperative processes by which their individual activities are directed and coordinated, or in the way in which passengers on a foundering ship share a common destiny remains to be seen. Although, ultimately there is no guarantee against political failure, there is good reason to hold that a politics based upon collective processes of deliberation among epistemically virtuous citizens will be able to avoid the worst political fates while engaging the mechanisms of its own improvement.

Notes

Chapter 1

1. *Los Angeles Times*, December 5, 1990.
2. Contrast the pessimism of C. B. Macpherson, expressed in the mid-60s: "Liberal-democratic nations can no longer expect to run the world, nor can they expect that the world will run to them" (1965, 3). See also the 1975 Trilateral Commission report which told of the "disintegration of the civil order, the breakdown of social discipline, the debility of leaders, and the alienation of citizens" (Crozier, Huntington, and Watanuki 1975, 2); cf. Huntington's foreword to Pharr and Putnam, eds. 2000.
3. Seyla Benhabib notes that neofascist movements are emerging "on a scale unprecedented since the end of World War II" (1996a, 3). For a current study of racist and nationalist movements in America, see Swain 2002.
4. Ibid.
5. I shall use the term *social pluralism* throughout to denote the fact of disagreement among citizens of contemporary democratic societies at the level of moral, religious, and philosophical essentials. *Social pluralism* is hence a purely descriptive term and must not be confused for overtly philosophical theses that are known as "pluralism."
6. From the common formula philosophy, where S and p are variables standing for subject and proposition respectively.

Chapter 2

1. The matter is further complicated by the recent rise of a view called "left-libertarianism." I cannot examine this view here; for a review of this literature, see Fried 2004.
2. Cf. Buchanan 1989, 854; Geuss 2002, 323; and Galston 2002, 3–4. For extended discussions, see Forst 2002, Ch. 2; and Gaus 2003, Ch. 1.
3. For suggestions of the former interpretation, see Nozick, who emphasizes "the fact of our separate existences" (1974, 33); Brian Barry, who speaks of "individual autonomous units" (1973, 166); and Bruce Ackerman, for whom political theory begins with "asocial monads" (1980, 100). The recent work of John Rawls is the main source of the practical reading of the Primacy of the Individual (Rawls 1985, 403ff).
4. I mention again that citations to Rawls's *A Theory of Justice* will be keyed to the Revised Edition of 1999 and will be designated by the abbreviation "TJ."
5. Rawls (1996, 13ff.) has employed the term "comprehensive doctrine" to describe what I am here calling a conception of the good.
6. In fact, many have claimed that the freedom of each to select and pursue his own conception of the good is the essence of liberty itself, as Mill does. Liberals need not take so strong a view.

7. Although several prominent liberals advance some version of this principle, there are others, such as Joseph Raz, who explicitly deny that the liberal state must be neutral. For other expressions of neutralism, see Nozick 1974; Ackerman, 1980; Kymlicka 1989; and Nagel 1987 and 1991 (Ch. 14). The concept of neutrality is widely criticized; see Beiner 1992 (Ch. 2); Barber 1984 (Part 1); Sandel 1982, 1984a, 1984b, and 1996; and Sher 1997.

8. Cf. Mill 1859, 121ff. Elsewhere, Mill claims that the principle that "each is the only safe guardian of his own rights and interests" is "one of those elementary maxims of prudence" (1861b, 245).

9. See, for example, Sunstein (1993b), who endorses a civic republican interpretation of the U.S. Constitution. He accordingly rejects liberalism but endorses a roughly liberal set of institutions and policies. One could argue that Raz and Sher similarly reject liberalism but endorse liberal policies; the same might be said of Mill, on certain interpretations.

10. Hegel and Heidegger are often named in this connection as well. See, for example, Taylor 1979, Ch. 2; and Bell 1993, *passim*.

11. Citations to Aristotle will employ the Bekker numbers, prefaced by abbreviations indicating the name of the work from which the citation is drawn. *NE* indicates the *Nicomachean Ethics* (Aristotle 1962); *P* indicates the *Politics* (Aristotle 1997). I shall leave the word *polis* untranslated as Ostwald's rendering ("state") is different from Simpson's ("city").

12. On these points, see Simpson 1998, 21f. and Miller 1995, Ch. 2.

13. Rawls writes, "a continuing shared understanding on one comprehensive religious, philosophical, or moral doctrine can be maintained *only* by the oppressive use of state power" (emphasis added). He calls this the "fact of oppression" (1996, 37).

14. Turning again to Rawls, "In the society of the Middle Ages, more or less united in affirming the Catholic faith, the Inquisition was not an accident; its suppression of heresy was needed to preserve that shared religious belief" (1996, 37).

15. See, for example, Mill's *On Liberty* for a most spirited defense of diversity and social toleration of diverse "experiments of living" as "not an evil, but a good" (1859, 62).

16. Lamentations over the term "communitarianism" are legion. See, for example, Sandel 1998b; Beiner 1992, 28f.; and MacIntyre 1998, 243–246.

17. See Elshtain 1995; Barber 1984; and especially Robert Putnam 1995.

18. See Etzioni, ed. 1998 for communitarian perspectives on the family, public space, crime, and education. See also Etzioni 1993; Etzioni 1996; Bellah, et al. 1991; Bellah, et al. 1985; and Galston 1990.

19. It is important to note here that, in the article just cited, Gutmann refers to the "communitarian" critique of liberalism. She is, however, discussing the work of Sandel, whom I have characterized as a civic republican, and not a communitarian in the sense I am employing the term.

20. Note that the main philosophers associated with the communitarian side of the liberal-communitarian debate—Sandel, Taylor, Walzer, MacIntyre—have not elected to add their signatures to Amitai Etzioni's "Responsive Communitarian Platform" (Etzioni, ed. 1998, xxv-xxxix).

21. Etzioni claims that the source of the "higher-order" principles is the "convictions held by many Americans" (1998, xv); however, he also has indicated that "the deontological position is most satisfactory" as a ground for higher-order values (1995, 20). It is not clear that Etzioni can with consistency appeal to deontology and maintain his communitarianism.

22. For a discussion of these possible misunderstandings, and an examination of the relation of theory to practice, see Beiner 1998, 10–13.

23. The ordinance was drafted by Catherine MacKinnon and Andrea Dworkin in 1983, and is reprinted in the Appendix to Dwyer 1995. The ordinance was vetoed by the mayor of Minneapolis and ruled unconstitutional by the district court of Indianapolis (a ruling upheld by the Supreme Court in 1986).

24. Sandel 1996 is an extended argument which attempts to demonstrate through an analysis of legal decisions the folly of trying to place the right prior to the good. See also Sandel 1989 for a similar argument focusing on abortion and sodomy legislation.

25. For a civic republican examination of the First Amendment which directly addresses the issue of pornography see Sunstein 1993a, Ch.7; see also Sunstein 2001b, Ch. 8 for a discussion of homosexuality. Sunstein characterizes his position as "Madisonian."

Chapter 3

1. Hence Waldron, "Like his empiricist counterparts in science, the liberal insists that intelligible justifications in social and political life must be available in principle for everyone, for society is to be understood by the individual mind, not by the tradition or sense of community. Its legitimacy and the basis of social obligation must be made out to each individual . . . " (1993, 44).

2. John Rawls (1985) introduced the idea of a "comprehensive" liberal theory. The term has since become standard. See Hampton 1993, 292–296; Gutmann 1985, 126; and especially Mulhall and Swift 1996, 249–258. It is important, however, to distinguish Rawls's term "comprehensive doctrine" from the idea of a "comprehensive liberalism"; a comprehensive doctrine is a theory of "what is of value in human life" which includes "ideals of personal character, as well as ideals of friendship and of familial and associational relationships, and much else that is to inform our conduct, and in the limit to our life as a whole" (1996, 13).

3. R. P. Wolff, a professed Kantian, accepts this conclusion and calls himself a "philosophical anarchist" (1998, xxviii). Here, I propose the modus tollens to Wolff's modus ponens: that Kant renders all workable political orders illegitimate is an objection to Kant's political theory.

4. According to R. P. Wolff, to obey a command is to act in accordance with it simply because it has been commanded (1998, 9). An autonomous agent may act in accordance with the commands of another, but he never acts simply because he has been commanded to do so (1998, 14).

5. Cf. Kant, "the right entails the authority to apply coercion to anyone who infringes it" (1797, 134).

6. Democracy is often offered as the solution to the dilemma between autonomy and political authority. However, Wolff persuasively argues that only "unanimous direct democracy" (1998, 22) actually succeeds in resolving the dilemma; but unanimous direct democracy cannot be achieved (1998, 26). Therefore, Wolff concludes, there could be no real resolution, and no state is legitimate.

7. Cf. Nozick, "Individuals have rights, and there are things no person or group may do to them (without violating their rights). So strong and far-reaching are these rights that they raise the question of what, if anything, the state and its officials may do. How much room do individual rights leave for the state?" (1974, ix). He continues, "The fundamental question of political philosophy, one that precedes questions about how the state should be organized, is whether there should be a state at all. Why not have anarchy?" (1974, 4).

8. Cf. Bentham, "*Evil* is pain, or the cause of pain. *Good* is pleasure, or the cause of pleasure" (1789, 685).

9. Hence Mill's Greatest Happiness Principle: "actions are right in proportion as they tend to promote happiness, wrong as they tend to produce the reverse of happiness" (1861a, 137).

10. Hence Bentham, "The Public Good ought to be the object of the legislator; General Utility ought to be the foundation of his reasonings" (1789, 685).

11. Hence Mill, "To have a right, then, is, I conceive, to have something which society ought to defend me in the possession of. If the objector goes on to ask why it ought, I can give him no other reason than general utility" (1861a, 189).

12. Barry has claimed that since Sidgwick's death, "nobody until Rawls has produced anything that represents a continuation of the cannon of political thought, traditionally conceived" (1996, 537); Nagel contends that Rawls is "the most important political philosopher of the twentieth century" (1999, 36). Nozick has registered the now famous compliment, "Political philosophers now must either work within Rawls' theory or explain why not" (1974, 183). Cf. Raz 1990, 61; Bell 1993, 2; Sandel 1998a, 184–185; and Shapiro 1999a, 3.

13. Cf. Rawls 1996, xiv–xv.

14. See R. P. Wolff 1977, Kukathas and Pettit 1990, and Talisse 2001, for exegetical treatments of Justice as Fairness.

15. Hume asks, "Where is the mutual agreement or voluntary association so much talked of?" (1748, 508). Ronald Dworkin raises a similar consideration when he asserts that "A hypothetical contract is not simply a pale form of an actual contract; it is no contract at all" (1973, 18).

16. Conversely, were one to show that a given principle would *not* be chosen in the original position, one would have demonstrated that the principle in question is not a valid principle of justice (TJ, 105–109).
17. This is a technical term, see TJ, 6–7; Cf. Rawls 1996, 11.
18. Rawls also identifies priority rules to govern the application of the principles (TJ, 266–267 and 36–40).
19. See page 303 of original edition; cf. page 54 of the revised edition.
20. This kind of response to the proposed objection has led some to conclude that Rawls's theory is simply too abstract to be of any political use. For this, see R. P. Wolff 1977, 195ff.; Miller, 1974; Barber 1975, 310ff. Pogge 1989 tries to draw out the specific policy implication of Rawls's view. On Pogge's reading of Rawls, see Crisp and Jamieson 2000.
21. This is evident in Locke: "To understand political power . . . we must consider what state all men are naturally in" (1689a, 218). See Fisk 1975 for an insightful discussion of Rawls and this aspect of contractarianism.
22. Hare 1973 argues that this view commits Rawls to ethical subjectivism.
23. See, for example, Dworkin 1973; Nagel 1973; Lyons 1975; R. P. Wolff 1977, Ch. XVI; Sandel 1982, Ch. 3; and Kukathas and Pettit 1990, Ch 2.
24. Cf. Dworkin 2000, 118.
25. See also Bell 1993; Barber 1984, Ch. 4; and Taylor 1990.

Chapter 4

1. See Talisse 2001 for a discussion of the details of political liberalism.
2. "It is the fact of reasonable pluralism that leads . . . to the idea of a political conception of justice and so to the idea of political liberalism" (Rawls 1996, xlvii).
3. See Rawls 1996, 36 for the distinction between "pluralism as such" and "reasonable pluralism."
4. "It is unreasonable for us to use political power, should we possess it, or share it with others, to repress comprehensive doctrines that are not unreasonable" (Rawls 1996, 61). Rawls suggests that it may be fully reasonable in some cases to use political power to repress unreasonable comprehensive doctrines.
5. Rawls himself does not specify what is involved in containing a doctrine, but note the discussions of the "political virtues" which a liberal regime must "strengthen" (1996, 195) through education (1996, 199).
6. Cf. Nagel 2001, 105–106.
7. Dworkin has put the point well: according to value pluralism, "values conflict . . . even if we get all the breaks" (2001, 78).
8. See Berlin 1969, li; Gray 2000a, 87–94; Galston 2002, 4–6; Keekes 2000; Baghramian and Ingram 2000; Lukes 2001, 53–54 for detailed formulations of the value pluralist thesis from which the above derives.
9. The inescapability of "choosing between absolute claims," leads us to place "immense value on the freedom to choose" (Berlin 1969, 168).
10. "Incompossible" is a technical term deriving from metaphysical discussions of moral logic; two states of affairs are incompossible when the possibility of one renders the other impossible.
11. Following Raz (1986), we may envision a state that simultaneously promotes all three options specified above, as well as many other good options, but does not claim that any of these is exclusively good or best. Such a state would certainly be engaged in something more than protecting negative liberty, but I cannot see how a value pluralist has the resources to argue that such a state would be unreasonable.
12. Kymlicka writes, "You can coerce someone into going to church and making the right physical movements, but you won't make someone's life better that way. It won't work, even if the coerced person is mistaken in her belief that praying to God is a waste of time. It won't work because a life only goes better if led from the inside (and some values can only be pursued from the inside)" (1989, 12).
13. I note once again Raz's (1986) pluralist argument for an autonomy-based perfectionist liberalism. Notice that Galston rejects Raz's proposal, claiming that it is insufficiently pluralist (2002, 20–27).

14. See for example, Stout 1988, 230; West 1985; West 1989, 206; Bernstein 1987, 541; Teichman 1989; and McCarthy 1990.
15. For Rorty's gloss on this passage in Rawls, see Rorty 1988, 180.
16. See Swain 2002 for current data. See also Mason 2002 for analysis of prolife radicalism.
17. See Swain and Nieli 2003 for interviews with ten white nationalist leaders; they invariably contend that they have good reasons and strong arguments for their views.
18. See, for example, Brian Barry (2001), who has produced a forceful liberal theory he calls "liberal equality."

Chapter 5

1. Unless otherwise specified, parenthetical references to Stephanus pages will refer to the *Republic* (Compiled in Plato 1997). The image of a ship is also found in Plato's *Statesman* (302a) and the *Euthydemus* (291d). Socrates raises a similar argument in the *Protagoras* (319b–320c).
2. See the account of how democracy comes to be in Book VIII of the *Republic* (555b ff.). Democracy arises out of a war between rich and poor in an oligarchy; when the poor (the many) win the war, democracy is instated.
3. Hence Socrates's famous plea: "Until philosophers rule as kings or those now called kings and leading men genuinely and adequately philosophize . . . cities will have no rest from evils . . . nor, I think, will the human race" (473c"–d).
4. In the *Republic*, democracy is superior only to the very worst constitution, namely, tyranny. However, note that the democratic man devolves into a tyrant and the democratic city generates tyranny (565d ff.; 571a ff.).
5. There are, of course, variations of this argument that claim to be democratic. For example, theorists such as Joseph Schumpeter and Walter Lippmann have posed what has come to be known as the "elitist" conception of democracy. According to the elitist view, "we define the democratic method as that institutional arrangement for arriving at political decisions in which individuals acquire the power to decide by means of a competitive struggle for the people's vote" (Schumpeter 1950, 83). See also Lippmann 1922, and more recently Posnor 2003.
6. The following discussion draws, with modifications, from Estlund 1993b.
7. Estlund employs the term "epistocracy" (1997, 183); I prefer "empistemarchy" since this conveys the idea of the *justified* or *de jure* rule of the knowers.
8. As shown in Chapter Two, Mill endorses the Epistemarchy Principle (1861b, 335–337).
9. On the idea of liberal "abstinence" from philosophical commitment, see also Larmore 1987, Ch. 4; Dworkin 1988, 196ff.; Nagel 1987; Nagel 1991, Ch. 14; Raz 1990; Hampton 1989; Hampton 1993; and Estlund 1998.
10. Hence Rawls, echoing Berlin, "there is no social world without loss" (1996, 197).
11. Similar characterizations are found in Bohman 1996, 1–3; Cohen 1989, 411–412; Gould 1988, 97; Gutmann and Thompson 1996, 26–33.
12. Note that Locke's *First Treatise* is directed against the works of Sir Robert Filmer, who argued that the authority of the king derived from God. Compare Socrates' claim that his philosophical kingship will require a "noble lie" establishing the justice of the rule of the guardians if it is to be stable (414c). We might think of Socrates' "myth of the metals" as a comprehensive doctrine by which (philosophical) monarchy is legitimated.
13. See R. Putnam 2000 for the most current data concerning the decline of civic associations. See also R. Putnam 1995; Barber 1998a; Elshtain 1995a; Beem 1999; O'Connell 1999; Bellah et al., 1985; Ehrenberg 1999; Dionne 1991; Etzioni 1993; Janowitz 1983; and People for the American Way, 1989. For recent information concerning public ignorance and incompetence, see the essays collected in Elkin and Soltan, eds. 1999; the essays collected in Marcus and Hanson, eds. 1993; Kelner 1990; Page 1996; Ferejohn, 1990; Iyengar 1991; Anderson 1998; and Somin 1998.
14. Major statements of the varieties of democratic antiliberalism can be found in Arato and Cohen 1994; Barber 1984; Barber 1998a; Barber 1998b; Beem 1999; Beiner 1992; Daggar 1997; Elshtain 1995a; Etzioni 1993; Etzioni 1996; Pettit 1997; Sandel 1996; Maynor 2003; and Honohan 2002.

15. See Mulhall and Swift 1996 for a comprehensive survey. Avineri and de-Shalit, eds. 1992 and Sandel, ed. 1984 compile many of the relevant articles. See also Kymlicka 1988; Kymlicka 1989a; Bell 1993; Caney 1992; Mulhall and Swift 1993; Walzer 1990; Buchanan 1989; Holmes 1993; Taylor 1989; Frazer and Lacey, 1993; V. Held 1987; V. Held, 1993; Etzioni, ed. 1995; and Etzioni, ed. 1998.

16. See Rawls 1996, Ch. VI; Rawls 1999; Gutmann and Thompson 1996; Gutmann and Thompson 1990; Gutmann and Thompson 1994; Cohen 1989; Cohen 1993; Cohen; 1996; Cohen 1998; Ackerman 1980; Ackerman 1989.

17. See Sandel 1996, 317ff.; Barber 1998a, Ch. 4; Barber 1998b, 13ff; Benhabib 1996b; and Young 2000.

18. Bohman and Rheg, eds. 1997, Elster, ed. 1998, and the first part of Benhabib, ed. 1996 contain all the major statements. See also Macado, ed. 1999; Dryzek 1990; Nino 1996; Bohman 1996; Gundersen 2000; Dryzek 2000; and Young 2000. Bohman (1998) and Freeman (2000) have written helpful survey articles.

19. There are interesting convergences across Anglo-American and Continental lines, as between Habermas's view of an "ideal speech situation," Cohen's "ideal deliberative procedure," and Rawls's "public reason." See Cohen 1989, and the exchange between Habermas (1995) and Rawls (1995). The convergence is lamented by Dryzek (2000).

20. Cohen explicitly claims that the deliberative model is an alternative to the aggregative; see Cohen 1996, 411 and Cohen 1998, 185–187.

21. See Rawls 1996, 243, n.32 for a discussion of how a "reasonable balance" of political values will "give a woman a duly qualified right to decide whether to end her pregnancy during the first trimester." See also Dworkin 1993b for an attempt to recast the abortion controversy into strictly political terms.

22. The attempt to demonstrate that a particular conception of reason is "sectarian" is question begging—one must employ reason (and thus presume a certain conception of reason) to construct the demonstration.

23. Recall Fukuyama: liberal democracy represents "the end point of mankind's ideological evolution" (1989, 4).

24. For example, Nozick's (1974, Ch. 7) and Dworkin's (2000, 330–331) criticisms of Rawls's difference principle.

25. Recall Rawls's "fact of oppression" (1996, 37).

26. See Cohen's discussion of Sandel (1998, 222–224).

27. See Barber 1984 for the earlier expression, which emphasizes participation and not explicitly deliberation.

Chapter 6

1. I follow the convention in citing Peirce's *Collected Papers*: (volume number. paragraph number).

2. See Estlund 1993b and Copp 1993.

3. For the analogy between grasping the Good and seeing the Sun, see 508b–c. *Theoria* is etymologically related to the idea of a spectator at a sporting event; a *theoros* is an "observer." It is the word from which "theater" and "theory" derive.

4. Appeals to "interests" and "preferences" have been shown to be subject to a host of complicating factors. See Estlund 1990; Sunstein 1993b, Ch. 6; Sunstein 2001b, 162–164; Nino 1996; and Benhabib 1996b, 71–74.

5. David Miller rejects epistemic views of deliberative democracy because he presumes that they must countenance "transcendent" standards of "justice or rightness" (2003, 185).

6. The taxonomy that follows builds upon discussions in Bohman 1998; Freeman 2000; Dryzek 2000, 173–174; List and Goodin 2001; and Goodin 2003, 91ff.

7. See Rawls on "public reason" (1999b); see also Cohen 1996 and Gutmann and Thompson 1996.

8. Rousseau is often cited as offering an epistemic conception. See Cohen 1986 for an early sketch of the epistemic view. Nino 1996 develops an epistemic deliberativism; the most sophisticated version, however, is found in the work of Estlund (1993a; 1993b; 1997; 1998).

9. Cf. Wiggins 1998 and Haack 1998, 8.
10. This is Misak's gloss on Peirce's "end of inquiry" view of truth. See also Misak 1991.
11. Hookway argues that the Peircean account of truth "can be held in conjunction with a realist or an anti-realist metaphysics" (2000, 77).
12. See Misak's gloss on this term (2000, 156; 2000, 167, n. 1).
13. Cf. Hilary Putnam's arguments against Habermas (1991, 229–232).
14. This seems to me to be Socrates' strategy in dealing with Thrasymachus in *Republic* Book I; See Roochnik (1990) for an interesting discussion. See Swain and Nieli 2003 for a series of interviews with leaders of neo-Nazi and other militant white-supremacist organizations; of particular import to us here is the fact that they all take themselves to have good reasons and evidence for their views.
15. Cf. Haack's discussion of the "many striking features" of scientific inquiry (1998, 106–107).
16. Cf. Stokes 1998; Przeworski 1998; Shapiro 1999b; and Young 2003.
17. See Mansbridge 1990; Honig 1993; Sanders 1997; Mouffe 2000; and Young 2003 for criticisms of consensus-based proposals. Not all deliberativisms are aimed at consensus; see Bohman 1996, Ch. 2; Dryzek 2000, Ch. 2; and Valadez 2001, Ch. 2.
18. Cf. Young, "Standards of political communication should be thought of as *virtues*" (2000, 80).
19. Although I endorse a virtue-theoretic account of deliberation or truth seeking, I need not endorse a full-blown virtue epistemology. I cannot treat these issues fully here, but see especially Blackburn 2001; Hookway 2000 and 2001; Axtell 2000; and Fairweather and Zagzebski 2001.
20. Cf. Dewey's description of the "morale" of inquiry (1939, 167) and van Eemeren and Grootendorst's "code of conduct" for participants in critical discussion (2004, Ch. 8).
21. Cf. Forst, "Democracy is the rule generally justified reasons" (2002, 123).
22. Cf. Misak's discussion of O'Niell's distinction between moral disagreement and moral disorientation (2000, 35).
23. Ian Shapiro brings this kind of objection against Gutmann and Thompson. Considering the case of the religious fundamentalist, Shapiro writes, "The Gutmann-Thompson view works only for those fundamentalists who also count themselves fallibilist democrats. That, I fear, is an empty class, destined to remain uninhabited" (Shapiro 2003, 26).
24. Gutmann and Thompson (1996, 17f.) raise a similar objection against the views of Habermas and Benhabib. See Benhabib 1996b, 77–79 for a response.

Chapter 7

1. See Gutmann and Thompson 1996; Nino 1996; Leib 2004.
2. Cf. Bartels 1996. See also Patterson's research regarding the 2000 election; just before election day only 38% of the voters he polled could correctly identify their favored candidate's position on crucial campaign issues (2002, 125). He concludes that "Issue awareness in 2000 may have been the lowest in modern times" (2002, 126).
3. The weakness of Posner's view should become more apparent once it is taken out of its third-person formulation and placed into a first-person context. Ask yourself: Are your own political views the outcome of sincere attempts to evaluate data and reasons, or are they simple expressions of your preferences?
4. See also Page 1996; Somin 1998; Iyengar 1991; Sunstein 1993a, Ch. 3; Jamieson and Waldman 2003; Elkin and Soltan 1999; and Chambers and Costain 2000.
5. See also Gastil 2000; McAfee 2004.
6. In Young's essay, the activist is male and the deliberativist is female. Young explains her decision to cast the characters in this way in a footnote (2003, 119 n.3). For clarity, I follow her use of the gender pronouns.
7. There are important questions that cannot be engaged here concerning the morality of activist tactics. Certain actions, such as physical assault, are obviously impermissible whereas others, such as nonviolent protest, are clearly permissible. Young stipulates that her activist opposes "intentional violence directed at others" and "serious" forms of property damage (2003, 105). For the sake of argument, I accept this characterization of the activist.

8. It is worth noting that certain versions of deliberative democracy are vulnerable to Young's activist criticisms. The objective here is to show that the view I have promoted is not.

9. A similar line of criticism is deployed in Przeworski 1998, Stokes 1998, and Sanders 1997.

10. The claim could be that all modes of communication are necessarily distorting and ideology laden. This might explain the lack of analysis, but it would render the activist's view self-referentially defeating.

11. I draw here from Swain and Nieli's (2003) collection of interviews with leaders of prominent racist, anti-Semitic, and white supremacist groups. The logical similarities between the position of Young's activist and that of many of these figures is striking. For example, William Pierce, the late author of *The Turner Diaries*, complains about the exclusive nature of existing institutions, describes his mission as "educational," advocates "resistance" and emphasizes the need to create new structures devoted to "communicating with people, to getting people to accept responsibility for what's happening in the world" (Swain and Nieli 2003, 272). Lisa Turner, the Women's Information Coordinator for the neo-Nazi World Church of the Creator, claims to be a "radical activist" aiming to "bring more racial awareness" to those who have been "brainwashed and propagandized" by the "power structure" (Swain and Nieli 2003, 258).

Works Cited

Ackerman, Bruce. 1980. *Social Justice in the Liberal State*. New Haven, CT: Yale University Press.

———. 1989. "Why Dialogue?" *Journal of Philosophy* 86: 16–27.

Ackerman, Bruce and James Fishkin. 2003. "Deliberation Day." In Fishkin and Laslett.

———. 2004a. "Righting the Ship of Democracy." *Legal Affairs* January/February 2004: 34–39.

———. 2004b. *Deliberation Day*. New Haven, CT: Yale University Press.

Allen, Anita and Milton Regan, eds. 1998. *Debating Democracy's Discontent*. New York: Oxford University Press.

Alterman, Eric. 2003. *What Liberal Media?* New York: Basic Books.

Anderson, Richard. 1998. "The Place of the Media in Popular Democracy." *Critical Review* 12, no. 4 (Fall): 481–500.

Arato, Andrew and Jean Cohen. 1994. *Civil Society and Political Theory*. Cambridge, MA: MIT Press.

Aristotle. 1962. *Nicomachean Ethics*. Martin Ostwald translation. New York: Prentice Hall.

———. 1997. *Politics*. Simpson translation. Chapel Hill: University of North Carolina Press.

Avineri, Shlomo, Avner de-Shalit, eds. 1992. *Communitarianism and Individualism*. New York: Oxford University Press.

Axtell, Guy. 2000. "Virtue Theory and the Fact/Value Problem." In *Knowledge, Belief, and Character*, Guy Axtell, ed. Lanham, MD: Rowman and Littlefield.

Baghramian, Maria and Attracta Ingram. 2000. "Introduction." In *Pluralism*, Baghramian and Ingram, eds. London: Routledge.

Barber, Benjamin. 1975. "Justifying Justice: Problems of Psychology, Politics, and Measurement in Rawls." In Daniels, ed.

———. 1984. *Strong Democracy*. Berkeley, CA: University of California Press.

———. 1998a. *A Place for Us*. New York: Hill and Wang.

———. 1998b. *A Passion for Democracy*. Princeton, NJ: Princeton University Press.

Barry, Brian. 1973. *The Liberal Theory of Justice*. New York: Oxford University Press.

———. 1996. "Political Theory Old and New." In *A New Handbook for Political Science*, Robert Goodin and Hans-Dieter Klingemann, eds. Cambridge, UK: Oxford University Press.

———. 2001. *Culture and Equality*. Cambridge, MA: Harvard University Press.

Bartels, Larry. 1996. "Uninformed Votes: Information Effects in Presidential Elections." *American Journal of Political Science* 40,no. 1:194–230.

Batstone, David and Eduardo Mendieta, eds. *The Good Citizen*. New York: Routledge.

Beem, Christopher. 1999. *The Necessity of Politics*. Chicago: University of Chicago Press.

Beiner, Ronald. 1992. *What's the Matter With Liberalism?* Berkeley: University of California Press.

———. 1998. "The Quest for a Post-Liberal Public Philosophy." In Allen and Regan, eds.

Bell, Daniel A. 1993. *Communitarianism and its Critics*. New York: Oxford University Press.

Bellah, Robert, et al. 1985. *Habits of the Heart*. Berkeley, CA: University of California Press.

———. 1991. *The Good Society*. New York: Knopf.

————. 1999. "The Ethics of Polarization in the United States and the World." In Batstone and Mendieta, eds.

Benhabib, Seyla. 1992a. *Situating the Self*. New York: Routledge.

————. 1992b. "Models of Public Space." In *Habermas and the Public Sphere*, Craig Calhoun, ed. Cambridge, MA: MIT Press.

————. 1996a. "The Democratic Moment and the Problem of Difference." In Benhabib, ed.

————. 1996b. "Toward a Deliberative Model of Democratic Legitimacy." In Benhabib, ed.

————, ed. 1996. *Democracy and Difference*. Princeton, NJ: Princeton University Press.

Berlin, Isaiah. 1969. "Two Concepts of Liberty." In *Four Essays on Liberty*. New York: Oxford University Press.

Bernstein, Richard. 1987. "One Step Forward, Two Steps Backward: Richard Rorty on Liberal Democracy and Philosophy." *Political Theory* 15: 538-563.

Bentham, Jeremy. 1789. *An Introduction to the Principles of Morals and Legislation*. In Cahn, ed.

Blackburn, Simon. 2001. "Reason, Virtue, and Knowledge." In Fairweather and Zagzebski, eds.

Bohman, James and William Rehg, eds. 1997. *Deliberative Democracy*. Cambridge, MA: MIT Press.

Bohman, James. 1996. *Public Deliberation*. Cambridge, MA: MIT Press.

————. 1998. "The Coming of Age of Deliberative Democracy." *The Journal of Political Philosophy* 6, no.4 (December): 400–425.

————. 1999. "Democracy as Inquiry, Inquiry as Democratic." *American Journal of Political Science* 43, no.2 (April): 590–607.

Brint, Michael and Weaver, William, eds. 1991. *Pragmatism in Law and Society*. Boulder, CO: Westview Press.

Buchanan, Allen. 1989. "Assessing the Communitarian Critique of Liberalism." *Ethics*, 99: 852–882.

Cahn, Steven, ed. 1997. *Classics of Modern Political Theory*. New York: Oxford University Press.

Cahoone, Lawrence. 2002. *Civil Society*. New York: Blackwell.

Caney, S. 1992. "Liberalism and Communitarianism: A Misconceived Debate." *Political Studies* 40: 273–290.

Carter, April and Geoffrey Stokes, eds. 1998. *Liberal Democracy and its Critics*. Cambridge, UK: Polity Press.

Chambers, Simone and Anne Costain, eds. 2000. *Democracy, Deliberation, and the Media*. Lanham, MD: Rowman and Littlefield.

Chomsky, Noam. 1989. *Necessary Illusions*. Boston: South End Press.

————. 1997. "Media Control: The Spectacular Achievements of Propaganda." *The Open Media Pamphlet Series*, no 2. New York: Seven Stories Press.

Cohen, Joshua. 1986. "An Epistemic Conception of Democracy." *Ethics* 97: 6–25.

————. 1989. "Deliberation and Democratic Legitimacy." In Bohman and Rehg, eds.

————. 1993. "Moral Pluralism and Political Consensus." In Copp, et al. eds.

————. 1996. "Procedure and Substance in Deliberative Democracy." In Bohman and Rehg, eds.

————. 1998. "Democracy and Liberty." In Elster, ed.

Conason, Joe. 2003. *Big Lies: The Right-Wing Propaganda Machine and How it Distorts the Truth*. New York: Thomas Dunne Books.

Copp, David, Jean Hampton, and John Roemer, eds. 1993. *The Idea of Democracy*. New York: Cambridge University Press.

Copp, David. 1993. "Could Political Truth be a Hazard for Democracy?" In Copp, et al. eds.

Corn, David. 2003. *The Lies of George W. Bush*. New York: Crown Books.

Coulter, Ann. 2003. *Slander: Liberal Lies About the American Right*. New York: Three Rivers Press.

Crenson, Matthew and Benjamin Ginsberg. 2002. *Downsizing Democracy*. Baltimore, MD: Johns Hopkins University Press.

Crisp, Roger and Dale Jamieson. 2000. "Egalitarianism and a Global Resource Tax: Pogge on Rawls." In Davion and Wolf, eds.

Crozier, Michel, Samuel P. Huntington, and Joji Watanuki. 1975. *The Crisis of Democracy*. New York: New York University Press.

Dahl, Robert. 1989. *Democracy and its Critics*. New Haven, CT: Yale University Press.

————. 1996. "Democratic Theory and Democratic Experience." In Benhabib, ed.

————. 1998. *On Democracy*. New Haven, CT: Yale University Press.

Daniels, Norman, ed. 1975. *Reading Rawls*. Oxford, UK: Basil Blackwell.

Dagger, Richard. 1997. *Civic Virtues*. New York: Oxford University Press.

Davion, Victoria and Clark Wolf, eds. 2000. *The Idea of a Political Liberalism: Essays on Rawls*. Lanham, MD: Rowman and Littlefield.

Dewey, John. 1938. *Logic: The Theory of Inquiry*. *The Later Works of John Dewey*, Vol. 12. Jo Ann Boydston, ed. Carbondale, IL: Southern Illinois University Press, 1988.

———. 1939. *Freedom and Culture*. *The Later Works of John Dewey*, Vol. 14. Jo Ann Boydston, ed. Carbondale, IL: Southern Illinois University Press, 1988.

Dionne, E. J. 1991. *Why Americans Hate Politics*. New York: Simon and Schuster.

Dryzek, John S. 1990. *Discursive Democracy*. Cambridge: Cambridge University Press.

———. 2000. *Deliberative Democracy and Beyond: Liberals, Critics, and Contestations*. New York: Oxford University Press.

Dworkin, Ronald. 1973. "The Original Position." In Daniels, ed.

———. 1978. "Liberalism." Reprinted in Dworkin, 1985.

———. 1981. "Do We Have a Right to Pornography?" Reprinted in Dworkin, 1985.

———. 1983. "What Justice Isn't." Reprinted in Dworkin, 1985.

———. 1985. *A Matter of Principle*. Cambridge, MA: Harvard University Press.

———. 1988. "Foundations of Liberal Equality." In *Equal Freedom: Selected Tanner Lectures on Human Values*, Stephen Darwall, ed. Ann Arbor: University of Michigan Press, 1995.

———. 1993a. "Liberty and Pornography." In Dwyer, ed.

———. 1993b. *Life's Dominion: An Argument about Abortion, Euthanasia, and Individual Freedom*. New York: Knopf.

———. 2001. "Do Liberal Values Conflict?" In Dworkin, Lila, and Silvers, eds.

Dworkin, Ronald, Mark Lila, and Robert B. Silvers, eds. 2001. *The Legacy of Isaiah Berlin*. New York: New York Review of Books.

Dworkin, Gerald. 1975. "Non-Neutral Principles." In Daniels, ed.

Dwyer, Susan, ed. 1995. *The Problem of Pornography*. Belmont, CA: Wadsworth.

Ehrenberg, John. 1999. *Civil Society*. New York: NYU Press.

Elkin, Stephen and Karol Edward Soltan, eds. 1999. *Citizen Competence and Democratic Institutions*. Pennsylvania: Penn State University Press.

Elshtain, Jean Bethke. 1995. *Democracy on Trial*. New York: Basic Books.

Elshtain, Jean Bethke and Christopher Beem. 1998. "Can this Republic be Saved?" In Allen and Regan, eds.

Elster, Jon. 1998. "Introduction." In Elster, ed. 1998.

Elster, Jon, ed. 1998. *Deliberative Democracy*. New York: Cambridge University Press.

Estlund, David. 1990. "Democracy Without Preference." *The Philosophical Review* Vol. 99, no. 3: 397–423.

———. 1993a. "Who's Afraid of Deliberative Democracy?" *Texas Law Review* 71: 1437–1477.

———. 1993b. "Making Truth Safe for Democracy." In Copp, Roemer, and Hampton, eds.

———. 1997. "Beyond Fairness and Deliberation." In Bohman and Rehg, eds.

———. 1998. "The Insularity of the Reasonable: Why Political Liberalism Must Admit the Truth." *Ethics* 108: 252–275.

Etzioni, Amitai. 1993. *The Spirit of Community*. New York: Simon and Schuster.

———. 1995. "Old Chestnuts and New Spurs." In Etzioni 1995.

———. 1996. *The New Golden Rule*. New York: Basic Books.

———. 1998. "Moral Dialogues." In Allen and Regan, eds.

———, ed. 1995. *New Communitarian Thinking*. Charlottesville: University Press of Virginia.

———, ed. 1998. *The Essential Communitarian Reader*. Lanham, MD: Rowman and Littlefield.

Fairweather, Abrol and Linda Zagzebski, eds. 2001. *Virtue Epistemology*. New York: Oxford University Press.

Ferejohn, John. 1990. "Information and the Electoral Process." In Ferejohn and Kuklinski, eds. *Information and the Democratic Process*. Chicago, IL: University of Illinois Press..

Fish, Stanley. 1999. "Mutual Respect as a Device of Exclusion." In Macado, ed.

Fishkin, James. 1991. *Democracy and Deliberation*. New Haven, CT: Yale University Press.

———. 1997. *The Voice of the People*. New Haven, CT: Yale University Press.

———. 1999. "Toward a Deliberative Democracy." In Elkin and Soltan, eds.

Fishkin, James and Peter Laslett, eds. 2003. *Debating Deliberative Democracy*. New York: Blackwell.

Fisk, Milton. 1975. "History and Reason in Rawls' Moral Theory." In Daniels, ed.

Forst, Rainer. 2002. *Contexts of Justice*. Berkeley: University of California Press.

Franken, Al. 2003. *Lies and the Lying Liars that Tell Them*. New York: E. P. Dutton.

Frazer, E. and N. Lacey. 1993. *The Politics of Community: A Feminist Critique of the Liberal-Communitarian Debate*. London: Harvester Wheatsheaf.

Freeman, Samuel, ed. 1999. *John Rawls: Collected Papers*. Cambridge, MA: Harvard University Press.

———. 2000. "Deliberative Democracy: A Sympathetic Comment." *Philosophy & Public Affairs* 29, no.4: 371–418.

Fried, Barbara H. 2004. "Left-Libertarianism: A Review Essay." *Philosophy & Public Affairs* 32, no.1: 66–92.

Friedman, Marilyn. 2000. "John Rawls and the Political Coercion of Unreasonable People." In Davion and Wolf, eds.

Fukuyama, Francis. 1989. "The End of History?" In *The National Interest*, Summer Issue.

Galston, William. 1990. "A Liberal-Democratic Case for the Two-Parent Family." Reprinted in Etzioni 1998.

———. 1991. "Rights Do Not Equal Rightness." *The Responsive Community* 1, no.4.

———. 1999. "Diversity, Toleration, and Deliberative Democracy." In Macedo, ed.

———. 2002. *Liberal Pluralism*. Cambridge: Cambridge University Press.

Gastil, John. 2000. *By Popular Demand*. Berkeley: University of California Press.

Gaus, Gerald. 2003. *Contemporary Theories of Liberalism*. London: Sage Publications.

George, Robert. 1999. "Law, Democracy, and Moral Disagreement." In Macedo, ed.

Geuss, Raymond. 2002. "Liberalism and its Discontents." *Political Theory* 30, no.3: 320–338.

Giddens, Anthony. 2000. *Runaway World*. New York: Routledge.

Goldberg, Bernard. 2003. *Bias: A CBS Insider Exposes How the Media Distort the News*. New York: Perennial Press.

Goodin, Robert E. 2000. "Democratic Deliberation Within." *Philosophy & Public Affairs* 29, no.1: 81–109.

———. 2003. *Reflective Democracy*. New York: Oxford University Press.

Gould, Carol. 1988. *Rethinking Democracy*. Cambridge: Cambridge University Press.

Gray, John. 1993. *Post-Liberalism*. New York: Routledge.

———. 2000a. *Two Faces of Liberalism*. New York: New Press.

———. 2000b. "Where Pluralists and Liberals Part Company." In Baghramian and Ingram, eds.

Gundersen, Adolf G. 2000. *The Socratic Citizen*. Lanham, MD: Lexington Books.

Gutmann, Amy and Dennis Thompson. 1990. "Moral Conflict and Political Consensus." *Ethics* 101: 64–88.

———. 1994. "Moral Disagreement in a Democracy." *Social Philosophy and Policy* 12: 87–110.

———. 1996. *Democracy and Disagreement*. Cambridge, MA: Belknap Press.

———. 2000. "Why Deliberative Democracy is Different." In Paul, Miller, and Paul, eds.

———. 2003. "Deliberative Democracy Beyond Process." In Fishkin and Laslett, eds.

Gutmann, Amy. 1985. "Communitarian Critics of Liberalism." *Philosophy and Public Affairs* 14, no.3: 308–322.

Haack, Susan. 1998. *Manifesto of a Passionate Moderate*. Chicago: University of Chicago Press.

Habermas, Jurgen. 1990. "Discourse Ethics." In Habermas, *Moral Consciousness and Communicative Action*. Cambridge, MA: MIT Press.

———. 1995. "Reconciliation Through the Public Use of Reason: Remarks on John Rawls' Political Liberalism." *Journal of Philosophy* 52: 109–131.

———. 1996. *Between Facts and Norms*. Cambridge, MA: MIT Press.

Hampton, Jean. 1989. "Should Political Philosophy be Done Without Metaphysics?" *Ethics* 99: 791–814.

———. 1993. "The Moral Commitments of Liberalism." In Copp, et al. eds.

Hardin, Russell. 1999. *Liberalism, Constitutionalism, and Democracy*. New York: Oxford University Press.

Hare, R. M. 1975. "Rawls's Theory of Justice." In Daniels, ed.

Held, Virginia. 1987. "Non-Contractual Society." *Canadian Journal of Philosophy*, 13: 111–138.

Holmes, Stephen. 1993. *The Anatomy of Antiliberalism*. Cambridge, MA: Harvard University Press.

Honig, Bonnie. 1993. *Political Theory and the Displacement of Politics*. Ithaca, NY: Cornell University Press.

Honohan, Iseult. 2002. *Civic Republicanism*. New York: Routledge.

Hook, Sidney. 2002. *Sidney Hook on Pragmatism, Democracy, and Freedom: The Essential Essays*. In Talisse and Tempio, eds. New York: Prometheus Books.

Hookway, Christopher. 2000. *Truth, Rationality, and Pragmatism*. New York: Oxford University Press.

———. 2001. "Epistemic *Akrasia* and Epistemic Virtue." In Fairweather and Zagzebski, eds.

Hume, David. 1748. "Of the Original Contract." In Cahn, ed.

Huntington, Samuel. 2000. "Foreword." In Pharr and Putnam, eds.

Iyengar, Shanto. 1991. *Is Anyone Responsible?* Chicago: University of Chicago Press.

———. 2000. "Media Effects: Paradigms for the Analysis of Local Television News." In Chambers and Costain, eds.

Jamieson, Kathlenn and Paul Waldman. 2003. *The Press Effect*. New York: Oxford University Press.

Janowitz, Morris. 1983. *The Reconstruction of Patriotism*. Chicago: University of Chicago Press.

Jefferson, Thomas, et al. 1776. *The Declaration of Independence*. In Cahn, ed.

Johnson, James. 1998. "Arguing for Deliberation: Some Skeptical Considerations." In Elster, ed.

Kant, Immanuel. 1781. "Appendix from the *Critique of Pure Reason*." In Reiss, ed.

———. 1785. *Foundations of the Metaphysics of Morals*. Beck translation. New York: Macmillan, 1985.

———. 1788. *Critique of Practical Reason*. Gregor translation. Cambridge: Cambridge University Press, 1997.

———. 1793. "Theory and Practice." In Reiss, ed.

———. 1797. *The Metaphysics of Morals*. In Reiss, ed.

Keekes, John. 2000. *Pluralism in Philosophy*. Ithaca, NY: Cornell University Press.

Kellner, Douglas. 1990. *Television and the Crisis of Democracy*. Boulder, CO: Westview Press.

Knight, Jack and James Johnson. 1997. "What Sort of Equality Does Deliberative Democracy Require?" In Bohman and Rehg, eds.

Kukathas, Chandran, and Phillip Pettit. 1990. *Rawls: A Theory of Justice and its Critics*. Stanford, CA: Stanford University Press.

Kymlicka, Will. 1988. "Liberalism and Communitarianism." *Canadian Journal of Philosophy* 18: 181–204.

———. 1989. *Liberalism, Community, and Culture*. New York: Oxford University Press.

———. 1998. "Liberal Egalitarianism and Civic Republicanism." In Allen and Regan, eds.

Langton, Rae. 1990. "Whose Right? Ronald Dworkin, Women, and Pornographers." Reprinted in Dwyer, ed.

Larmore, Charles. 1987. *Patterns of Moral Complexity*. Cambridge: Cambridge University Press.

Leib, Ethan J. 2004. *Deliberative Democracy in America*. College Park: Penn State University Press.

Lippmann, Walter. 1922. *Public Opinion*. New York: Free Press.

List, Christian and Robert Goodin. 2001. "Epistemic Democracy: Generalizing the Condorcet Jury Theorem." *The Journal of Political Philosophy* 9, no.3: 277–306.

Locke, John. 1689a. *Second Treatise of Government*. Reprinted in Cahn, ed.

———. 1689b. *A Letter Concerning Toleration*. Reprinted in Cahn, ed.

Lukes, Stephen. 1991. *Moral Conflicts and Politics*. New York: Oxford University Press.

———. 2001. "An Unfashionable Fox." In Drowkin, Lila, and Silvers, eds.

Luskin, Robert and James Fishkin. 2002. "Deliberation and 'Better Citizens'." Unpublished paper.

Lyons, David. 1975. "Nature and Soundness of the Contract and Coherence Arguments." In Daniels, ed.

Macado, Stephen, ed. 1999. *Deliberative Politics*. New York: Oxford University Press.

MacIntyre, Alasdair. 1998. "Politics, Philosophy, and the Common Good." *The MacIntyre Reader*, Kelvin Knight, ed. South Bend, IN: University of Notre Dame Press..

MacKinnon, Catherine. 1987. "Francis Biddle's Sister: Pornography, Civil Rights, and Speech." Reprinted in Dwyer, ed.

Macpherson, C. B. 1965. *The Real World of Democracy*. New York: Oxford University Press.

Mansbridge, Jane. 1983. *Beyond Adversary Democracy*. Chicago: University of Chicago Press.

———. 1990. "Feminism and Democracy." *The American Prospect* 1: 126–139.

———. 1999. "On the Idea that Participation Makes Better Citizens." In Elkin and Soltan, eds.

Marcus, George E. and Russell L. Hanson, eds. 1993. *Reconsidering the Democratic Public.* College Park, PA: The Pennsylvania State University Press.

Mason, Carol 2002. *Killing For Life.* Ithaca, NY: Cornell University Press.

Maynor, John W. 2003. *Republicanism in the Modern World.* Cambridge, UK: Polity Press.

McAfee, Noelle. 2004. "Three Models of Democratic Deliberation." *Journal of Speculative Philosophy* 18, no.1: 44–59.

McCarthy, Thomas. 1990. "Private Irony and Public Decency: Richard Rorty's New Pragmatism." *Critical Inquiry* 16 (Winter).

Mill, John Stuart. 1991. *On Liberty and Other Essays.* New York: Oxford University Press.

———. 1861a. *Utilitarianism.* In Mill 1991.

———. 1861b. *Considerations on Representative Government.* In Mill 1991.

———. 1859. *On Liberty.* In Mill, 1991.

Miller, Richard. 1974. "Rawls and Marxism." In Daniels, ed.

Miller, Fred, Jr. 1995. *Nature, Justice, and Rights in Aristotle's Politics.* New York: Oxford University Press.

Miller, David. 2003. "Deliberative Democracy and Social Choice." In Fishkin and Laslett, eds.

Misak, Cheryl. 1991. *Truth and the End of Inquiry.* New York: Oxford University Press.

———. 2000. *Truth, Politics, Morality.* New York: Routledge.

———. 2004. "Making Disagreement Matter." *Journal of Speculative Philosophy* 18, no.1: 9–22.

Morris, Dick. 2000. *Vote.Com.* New York: Renaissance Books.

Mouffe, Chantal. 2000. *The Democratic Paradox.* New York: Verso.

Mulhall, Stephen and Adam Swift. 1993. "Liberalisms and Communitarianisms: Whose Misconception?" *Political Studies* 41, no. 4:650–656.

———. 1996. *Liberals and Communitarians.* Second Edition. Oxford: Blackwell Publishers.

Nagel, Thomas. 1973. "Rawls on Justice." In Daniels, ed.

———. 1987. "Moral Conflict and Political Legitimacy." *Philosophy & Public Affairs* 16: 215–240.

———. 1991. *Equality and Partiality.* New York: Oxford University Press.

———. 1999. "Justice, Justice Shalt Thou Pursue." *New Republic*, October 25: 36–41.

———. 2001. "Pluralism and Coherence." In Dworkin, Lila, and Silvers, eds.

Nino, Carlos. 1996. *The Constitution of Deliberative Democracy.* New Haven, CT: Yale University Press.

Norris, Pippa. 2000. "The Impact of Television on Civic Malaise." In Pharr and Putnam, eds.

Nozick, Robert. 1974. *Anarchy, State, and Utopia.* New York: Basic Books.

Nussbaum, Martha. 1997. "The Feminist Critique of Liberalism." In *Sex and Social Justice.* New York: Oxford University Press, 1999.

O'Connell, Brian. 1999. *Civil Society.* Boston: Tufts University Press.

O'Reilly, Bill. 2003. *The No Spin Zone.* New York: Broadway Books.

Page, Benjamin. 1996. *Who Deliberates? Mass Media in Modern Democracy.* Chicago: University of Chicago Press.

Palast, Greg., 2003. *The Best Democracy Money Can Buy.* New York: Plume Press.

Patterson, Thomas E. 2002. *The Vanishing Voter.* New York: Knopf.

Paul, Ellen Frankel, Fred Miller, and Jeffrey Paul, eds. 2000. *Democracy.* Cambridge: Cambridge University Press.

Peirce, Charles Sanders. 1931–1958. *Collected Papers.* Hartshorne, Weiss, and Burks, eds. Cambridge, MA: Harvard University Press.

People For the American Way. 1989. *Democracy's Next Generation.* Washington, D. C.: People for the American Way Publications.

Pettit, Philip. 1997. *Republicanism.* New York: Oxford University Press.

———. 2003. "The Discursive Dilemma and Republican Theory." In Fishkin and Laslett, eds.

Pharr, Susan and Robert Putnam, eds. 2000. *Disaffected Democracies.* Princeton, NJ: Princeton University Press.

Plato. 1997. *Plato: Complete Works.* Edited by John Cooper. Indianapolis, IN: Hackett.

Pogge, Thomas. 1989. *Realizing Rawls.* Ithaca, NY: Cornell University Press.

Posner, Richard. 2003. *Law, Pragmatism, and Democracy.* Cambridge, MA: Harvard University Press.

———. 2004. "Smooth Sailing." *Legal Affairs* January/February 2004: 41–42.

Przeworski, Adam. 1998. "Deliberation and Ideological Domination." In Elster, ed.

Putnam, Hilary. 1991. "A Reconsideration of Deweyan Democracy." In Brint and Weaver, eds.

Putnam, Robert. 1993. *Making Democracy Work*. Princeton, NJ: Princeton University Press.

———. 1995. "Bowling Alone: America's Declining Social Capital." *Journal of Democracy* 6, no. 1 (January): 65–78.

———. 2000. *Bowling Alone: The Collapse and Renewal of American Community*. New York: Simon and Schuster.

Rawls, John. 1975. "Fairness To Goodness." Reprinted in Freeman, ed.

———. 1985. "Justice as Fairness: Political not Metaphysical." Reprinted in Freeman, ed.

———. 1989. "The Domain of the Political and Overlapping Consensus." Reprinted in Freeman, ed.

———. 1996. *Political Liberalism*. New York: Columbia University Press.

———. 1999a. *A Theory of Justice*. Revised Edition. Cambridge, MA: Harvard University Press. Original edition, Cambridge, MA: Harvard University Press, 1971.

———. 1999b. *The Law of Peoples*. Cambridge, MA: Harvard University Press.

Raz, Joseph. 1986. *The Morality of Freedom*. New York: Oxford University Press.

———. 1990. "Facing Diversity: The Case of Epistemic Abstinence." In *Ethics in the Public Domain*. New York: Oxford University Press, 1994.

Reiss, Hans ed. 1970. *Kant: Political Writings*. Cambridge: Cambridge University Press.

Richardson, Henry. 2002. *Democratic Autonomy*. New York: Oxford University Press.

Roochnik, David. 1990. *The Tragedy of Reason*. New York: Routledge.

Rorty, Richard. 1987. "Science as Solidarity" In Rorty 1991a.

———. 1988. "The Priority of Democracy to Philosophy." In Rorty 1991a.

———. 1989. *Contingency, Irony, and Solidarity*. Cambridge: Cambridge University Press.

———. 1991a *Objectivity, Relativism, and Truth*. Cambridge: Cambridge University Press.

———. 1996. "Idealizations, Foundations, and Social Practices." In Benhabib, ed.

———. 1997. "Religious Faith, Intellectual Responsibility, and Romance." In Rorty 1999.

———. 1998a. *Achieving Our Country: Leftist Thought in Twentieth-Century America*. Cambridge, MA: Harvard University Press.

———. 1998b. "A Defense of Minimalist Liberalism." In Allen and Regan, eds.

———. 1999. *Philosophy and Social Hope*. New York: Penguin.

Sandel, Michael. 1982. *Liberalism and the Limits of Justice*. Cambridge: Cambridge University Press.

———. 1984a. "Morality and the Liberal Ideal." In *New Republic* 7, May.

———. 1984b. "The Procedural Republic and the Unencumbered Self." In Avineri and de-Shalit, eds.

———. 1989. "Moral Argument and Liberal Toleration: Abortion and Homosexuality." In Etzioni 1995.

———. 1996. *Democracy's Discontent*. Cambridge, MA: Harvard University Press.

———. 1998a. "A Response to Rawls's Political Liberalism." Appendix to the second edition of *Liberalism and the Limits of Justice*. Cambridge: Cambridge University Press.

———. 1998b. "The Limits of Communitarianism." Preface to the second edition of *Liberalism and the Limits of Justice*. Cambridge: Cambridge University Press.

———. 1998c. "Reply to Critics." In Allen and Regan, eds.

———, ed. 1984. *Liberalism and Its Critics*. New York: New York University Press.

Sanders, Lynn. 1997. "Against Deliberation." In *Political Theory* 25, no.3: 347–376.

Schumpeter, Joseph. 1950. *Capitalism, Socialism, and Democracy*. In Philip Green, ed. *Democracy*. Atlantic Highlands, NJ: Humanities Press, 1993.

Shapiro, Ian. 1999a. *Democratic Justice*. New Haven, CT: Yale University Press.

———. 1999b. "Enough of Deliberation." In Macedo, ed.

———. 2003. *The State of Democratic Theory*. Princeton, NJ: Princeton University Press.

Sher, George. 1997. *Beyond Neutrality*. New York: Cambridge University Press.

Shue, Henry. 1980. *Basic Rights*. Princeton, NJ: Princeton University Press.

Simpson, Peter. 1990. "Making the Citizens Good: Aristotle's City and its Contemporary Relevance." *The Philosophical Forum*, XXII, no.2: 149–166.

———. 1998. *A Philosophical Commentary on the Politics of Aristotle*. Chapel Hill: University of North Carolina Press.

Skocpol, Theda. 2003. *Diminished Democracy*. Norman: University of Oklahoma Press.

Somin, Illya. 1998. "Voter Ignorance and the Democratic Ideal." *Critical Review* 12, no.4: 413–458.

Stokes, Susan C. 1998. "Pathologies of Deliberation." In Elster, ed.

Stout, Jeffrey. 1988. *Ethics After Babel*. Boston: Beacon Press.

———. 2004. *Democracy and Tradition*. Princeton, NJ: Princeton University Press.

Sunstein, Cass. 1993a. *Democracy and the Problem of Free Speech*. New York: Free Press.

———. 1993b. *The Partial Constitution*. Cambridge, MA: Harvard University Press.

———. 2001a. *Republic.com*. Princeton, NJ: Princeton University Press.

———. 2001b. *Designing Democracy*. New York: Oxford University Press.

———. 2003a. "The Law of Group Polarization." In Fishkin and Laslett, eds.

———. 2003b. *Why Societies Need Dissent*. Cambridge, MA: Harvard University Press.

Swain, Carol. 2002. *The New White Nationalism in America*. Cambridge: Cambridge University Press.

Swain, Carol and Russ Nieli, eds. 2003. *Contemporary Voices of White Nationalism*. Cambridge: Cambridge University Press.

Talisse, Robert. 2001. *On Rawls*. Belmont, CA: Wadsworth.

Taylor, Charles. 1979. *Hegel and Modern Society*. Cambridge: Cambridge University Press.

———. 1989. "Cross Purposes: The Liberal-Communitarian Debate." In Taylor 1995.

———. 1990. *Sources of the Self*. Cambridge, MA: Harvard University Press.

———. 1995. *Philosophical Arguments*. Cambridge, MA: Harvard University Press.

Teichman, Jenny. 1989. "Don't Be Cruel or Reasonable." *New York Times Book Review*, April 23, 1989.

Tocqueville, Alexis de. 1835. *Democracy in America*, Vol. 1. In Cahn, ed.

Tsagarousianou, Roza, ed. 1998. *Cyberdemocracy*. New York: Routledge.

Unger, Roberto. 1998. *Democracy Realized*. London: Verso.

van Eemeren, Frans H. and Rob Grootendorst. 2004. *A Systematic Theory of Argumentation*. Cambridge: Cambridge University Press.

Valadez, Jorge M. 2001. *Deliberative Democracy, Political Legitimacy, and Self-Determination in Multicultural Societies*. Boulder, CO: Westview Press.

Waldron, Jeremy. 1993. *Liberal Rights*. Cambridge: Cambridge University Press.

Walzer, Michael. 1990. "The Communitarian Critique of Liberalism." In Etzioni, 1995.

Weinshall, Matthew. 2003. "Means, Ends, and Public Ignorance in Habermas's Theory of Democracy." *Critical Review* 15, no.1–2 and 23–58.

West, Cornel. 1985. "The Politics of American Neo-Pragmatism." In John Rajchman and Cornel West, eds. *Post-Analytic Philosophy*. New York: Columbia University Press, 1985.

———. 1989. *The American Evasion of Philosophy*. Madison: University of Wisconsin Press.

Wiggins, David. 1998. "C. S. Peirce: Belief, Truth, and Going From the Known to the Unknown." In *Pragmatism*, Cheryl Misak, ed. Calgary, Alberta: University of Calgary Press.

Wilhelm, Anthony G. 2000. *Democracy in the Digital Age*. New York: Routledge.

Williams, Bernard. 2002. *Truth and Truthfulness*. Princeton, NJ: Princeton University Press.

Wolff, Jonathan. 1998. "John Rawls: Liberal Democracy Revisited." In Carter and Stokes, eds.

Wolff, Robert Paul. 1970. *In Defense of Anarchism*. New York: Harper and Row.

———. 1977. *Understanding Rawls*. Princeton, NJ: Princeton University Press.

———. 1998. *In Defense of Anarchism*. Revised Edition. Berkeley, CA: University of California Press.

Young, Iris Marion. 2000. *Inclusion and Democracy*. New York: Oxford University Press.

———. 2003. "Activist Challenges to Deliberative Democracy." In Fishkin and Laslett, eds.

Zakaria, Fareed. 2003. *The Future of Freedom*. New York: Norton.

Index

159